T0316570

Cambridge Elements ≡

Elements in Eighteenth-Century Connections
edited by
Eve Tavor Bannet
University of Oklahoma
Rebecca Bullard
University of Reading

MARY PRINCE, SLAVERY, AND PRINT CULTURE IN THE ANGLOPHONE ATLANTIC WORLD

Juliet Shields
University of Washington, Seattle

CAMBRIDGE
UNIVERSITY PRESS

CAMBRIDGE
UNIVERSITY PRESS

University Printing House, Cambridge CB2 8BS, United Kingdom

One Liberty Plaza, 20th Floor, New York, NY 10006, USA

477 Williamstown Road, Port Melbourne, VIC 3207, Australia

314–321, 3rd Floor, Plot 3, Splendor Forum, Jasola District Centre,
New Delhi – 110025, India

79 Anson Road, #06–04/06, Singapore 079906

Cambridge University Press is part of the University of Cambridge.

It furthers the University's mission by disseminating knowledge in the pursuit of education, learning, and research at the highest international levels of excellence.

www.cambridge.org
Information on this title: www.cambridge.org/9781108791656
DOI: 10.1017/9781108866392

© Juliet Shields 2021

First published 2021

A catalogue record for this publication is available from the British Library.

ISBN 978-1-108-79165-6 Paperback
ISSN 2632-5578 (online)
ISSN 2632-556X (print)

Mary Prince, Slavery, and Print Culture in the Anglophone Atlantic World

Elements in Eighteenth-Century Connections

DOI:10.1017/9781108866392
First published online: April 2021

Juliet Shields
University of Washington, Seattle
Author for correspondence: Juliet Shields, js37@uw.edu

Abstract: This study examines a network of writers that coalesced around the publication of *The History of Mary Prince* (1831), which recounts Prince's experiences as an enslaved person in the West Indies and the events that brought her to seek assistance from the Anti-Slavery Society in London. It focuses on the three writers who produced the text – Mary Prince, Thomas Pringle, and Susanna Moodie – with glances at their proslavery opponent, James MacQueen, and their literary friends and relatives. The *History* connects the Black Atlantic, a diasporic formation created through the colonial trade in enslaved people, with the Anglophone Atlantic, created through British migration and colonial settlement. It also challenges Romantic ideals of authorship as an autonomous creative act and the literary text as an aesthetically unified entity. Collaborating with Prince on the *History*'s publication impacted Moodie's and Pringle's attitudes toward slavery and shaped their own accounts of migration and settlement.

Keywords: slavery, migration, authorship, print, Atlantic

ISBNs:9781108791656 (PB), 9781108866392 (OC)
ISSNs:2632-5578 (online), 2632-556X (print)

Contents

1 Introduction: Mary Prince and the Romantic Atlantic World

In the past two decades, *The History of Mary Prince* (1831) has attained the central place in the study of Romantic-era British literature that it richly deserves as one of a handful of first-person accounts of the experience of enslavement from this period. Its centrality is indicative of the gradual transformation of Romanticism as a field of study that arguably has been hampered by the extent to which Romantic ideology still delimits our understandings of authorship and the literary work. When, in 1983, Jerome McGann's *The Romantic Ideology* powerfully charged scholarship on Romanticism with uncritically replicating Romantic poets' representations of their works as autonomous, original, aesthetically unified acts of self-expression that transcend the world of politics, the Romantic canon still consisted of the so-called Big Six (Blake, Byron, Coleridge, Keats, Shelley, and Wordsworth). With critical race studies still an emergent field, McGann did not consider that in uncritically replicating Romantic aesthetics, scholarship also unthinkingly perpetuated the canonization of elite white male poets. But it is nonetheless true that Romantic ideology, the celebration of the poet as an autonomous genius and the literary work as an original and transcendent aesthetic entity, has perhaps made Romanticism somewhat slower than the contiguous fields of eighteenth-century and Victorian literature to recognize and account for the ways that aesthetics can be not just politicized but also racialized – and can serve as an excuse for racial exclusion.

In the years since the publication of McGann's book, scholars have begun to examine Romantic literature's investments in and critiques of slavery and imperialism, including the participation of some of its major figures – Coleridge, Southey, More, and Baubauld – in the efforts to abolish the slave trade and colonial slavery (e.g., Thomas, 2000; Carey, 2005; Kitson, 2007; Bohls, 2014). But the writings of enslaved peoples remain marginalized in these discussions, in part because they can be difficult to access. Since its publication in 2000 in an expensive paperback version edited by Sara Salih, *The History of Mary Prince* has been central to the ongoing transformation of a field from which Black and Indigenous perspectives are still too often missing. Prince's *History*, which recounts her life as an enslaved person in the West Indies and the events that brought her to seek assistance from the Anti-Slavery Society in London, could not be farther from Wordsworth's recollections in tranquility or Keats's negative capability. Dictated to Susanna Strickland, an obscure contributor to fashionable magazines, buttressed by paratext written by minor Scottish poet Thomas Pringle, and incorporating testimony from other abolitionists, *The History of Mary Prince* challenges Romantic ideals of authorship as an autonomous creative act and of the literary text as an aesthetically unified entity.[1]

Mary Prince, Slavery, and Print Culture in the Anglophone Atlantic World provides a new context for understanding the significance of Prince's *History* by tracing its impact on British settler colonial writing. Whereas previous scholars have emphasized the *History*'s mediation by white abolitionist writers, calling into question Prince's agency as an author and the authenticity of her narrative, this study explores the impact of the *History* on those writers, suggesting that Prince was not merely a pawn in their struggles but an author from whose work they learned and whose narrative they imitated. And whereas previous studies have portrayed Prince's *History* as a narrative from the imperial outskirts that found an audience in Britain's metropolitan literary center, this study positions it as a metropolitan publication that reverberated through the peripheries of empire. It situates *The History of Mary Prince* at the center of a network of little-known Romantic-era migrant writers, focusing primarily on the three who produced the text – Mary Prince, Thomas Pringle, and Susanna Strickland Moodie – with glances at their most vocal proslavery opponent, James MacQueen, and their literary friends and relatives. This literary network illustrates the geographic and literary interconnections between the Black Atlantic world (Gilroy, 1995), a diasporic formation created through the colonial trade in enslaved people, and an Anglophone Atlantic world created through British migration and settlement. Indeed, the settler colonial Anglophone Atlantic was not merely connected to the Black Atlantic but built upon it, as enslavement of Black and Indigenous peoples was central to British settler colonial endeavors.

The network of migrant writers that coalesced around the publication of *The History of Mary Prince* traversed the reaches of the Atlantic world: Prince was bought and sold throughout the British West Indies before accompanying her enslavers Mr. and Mrs. Wood to London; Pringle left Scotland for South Africa, returning to London six years later; Strickland Moodie settled permanently in Upper Canada, and MacQueen made his fortune as a plantation overseer in Grenada before returning to Scotland. Including Prince, an enslaved person, in the category of "migrant writers" raises questions about how far her experiences of mobility can be compared to those of settlers or sojourners in the British colonies. While Prince's movements were largely dictated by her enslavers, it is important not to overlook

---

[1] It is difficult to avoid confusion in referring to a writer who published under both her maiden and married names. I generally use "Strickland Moodie" to refer to Susanna, which has the advantage of distinguishing her from her husband, John Moodie, unless I am writing specifically about her life and work before her marriage, including her time working on *The History of Mary Prince*, when I refer to her simply as "Strickland."

the agency that she did exert when she could. Often, Prince had no say in her journeys from one household or one island to another. But she certainly had preferences about where she lived and by whom she was enslaved, and she sought to realize those preferences. She relates that while she was enslaved by Mr. D– in Bermuda, she "felt a great wish to go" to Antigua and asked Mr. D– "to let me go in Mr Wood's service" (2000, p. 25). While this was undoubtedly a choice between two evils, it is one of several times that Prince describes exercising agency within the confines of slavery. Similarly, when she declares herself "willing to come to England" with Mr. and Mrs. Wood, she implies that she had some choice in the matter, and possibly the option not to go. As David Eltis has argued (2002), coerced and free migration form a continuum; they are not stark oppositions. A married woman, such as Strickland Moodie, whose husband decided against her wishes to emigrate to the colonies, may have felt deprived of agency, and a displaced tenant farmer who could not find work that would enable him to feed his children may have felt that emigration was his only option. But compared to enslaved peoples, colonial settlers and sojourners had unbounded agency.

In including Prince in the category of "migrant writers," then, I do not want to efface the vast differences between her experiences of mobility and those of white settlers and sojourners. But I do want to argue that her account of her movements in *The History of Mary Prince* distinguishes it from earlier male-authored slave narratives and influenced the accounts that Strickland Moodie and Pringle would go on to write of their own migrations. Prince's slave narrative, in short, shaped the emergent genre of the migrant narrative, an autobiographical account of migration and settlement. Like slave narratives, migrant narratives tend to be heterogeneous compilations, often written by more than one author even when the work appeared under a single name. Their multiauthored and multi-generic assemblages display a repetitiousness that worked to legitimate their representations, and their aims are pedagogical rather than aesthetic.

Ann Laura Stoler suggests the value of studying migrant writers when she observes that "research that begins with people's movements rather than with fixed polities opens up more organic histories that are not compelled by originary narratives designed to show the 'natural' teleology of future nations, later republics, and future states" (2001, p. 862). Beginning with fixed parameters, whether national, temporal, or literary historical, predetermines which writers we can study and which we must ignore. Following the movements of writers who lived and worked transnationally allows us to trace literary connections that reveal the contingency of the parameters through which we organize literary study.

Migrant writers do not fit easily into the national traditions that have long structured our discipline and that are only now beginning to give way to categories such as "global Anglophone" and "world literature." Pringle has been dubbed "the father of South African poetry" – a title Indigenous poets have rightly problematized – but his contributions to Scottish and British literary history have received much less attention.[2] Similarly, Susanna Strickland is virtually unknown to scholars of British Romantic literature compared to her sister Agnes Strickland, who remained in England, but under her married name, Susanna Moodie, she occupies a prominent place in the canon of early Canadian writers. Prince has been absorbed into British Romantic studies as scholars have begun to explore the centrality of slavery and abolition to the literature and culture of the period. But just as important aspects of Pringle's and Moodie's identities and work are lost if we understand them only as South African or Canadian, so we limit our understanding of Prince's by reading her narrative only in relation to Black British traditions *or* in the context of Caribbean literary culture, as Carole Boyce Davies (2002), Sandra Pouchet Paquet (2002), and Merinda K. Simmons (2009) have done.

I do not mean to argue simply that we should situate migrant writers in the literary culture of their points of origin as well as their destinations. Rather, I want to suggest that national traditions are inadequate containers within which to sort and place these writers. Scholars have already recognized this inadequacy in the case of Prince's *History* and other works by formerly enslaved people such as Olaudah Equiano's *Interesting Narrative* (1794) and Ottobah Cugoano's *Thoughts and Sentiments* (1787). These texts are generally read as products of the formation that Paul Gilroy terms the Black Atlantic. Gilroy (1995) has shown that diasporic Black cultures from around the Atlantic basin have closer ties to each other than to the nation-states within which they are situated. He envisions "the Atlantic as one single, complex unit of analysis" that might be used "to produce an explicitly transnational and intercultural perspective" of Black literature and culture (p. 15).

If the Black Atlantic was created as a diasporic formation through the trade in enslaved people, we might imagine an Anglophone Atlantic created through what James Belich has described as a "Settler Revolution" – a wave of British and Irish emigration spurred by the American and French Revolutions in the late eighteenth century and the Industrial Revolution in the early nineteenth (2009, p. 9). In arguing that the works of settler colonial writers are better understood within this diasporic formation than in terms of national literary traditions, I do

---

[2] On Indigenous challenges to Pringle's paternity claim, see Pereira and Chapman, 1989, pp. xi–xvi. Angus Calder (1982) and Sarah Sharp (2019) have explored connections between Pringle's Scottish and South African poems.

not mean to suggest that the experiences of settlers in South Africa were the same as those of settlers in Upper Canada or Australia, or those of sojourners in Brazil or Jamaica. Rather, I argue that taking "the Atlantic as one single, complex unit of analysis," as Gilroy does, allows us to see commonalities in the works of these writers that we miss when we relegate them to national traditions. These commonalities are both formal – a predilection for the genre of the sketch, for instance – and ideological, including assumptions about racial and cultural difference. Situating settler colonial writers in the context of the Anglophone Atlantic, a diasporic formation that they participated in creating, enables us to see them as belonging to a shared literary tradition that transcends the nation-state.

The writers I discuss here demonstrate that the Anglophone Atlantic inter-sected with and to a large extent was sustained by the Black Atlantic. Voluntary migration is motivated not only by "push" factors such as war, economic insecurity, or persecution at home but also by "pull" factors – the lure of greater opportunities, resources, and rights elsewhere. And for Britons in the eighteenth and nineteenth centuries, these possibilities abroad were often predicated on direct or mediated participation in the African slave trade and on the displace-ment and exploitation of Indigenous peoples. British migration throughout the Atlantic world inevitably entailed encounters with racial difference. Responses to these encounters varied greatly. There are considerable internal tensions and contradictions in Pringle's and Strickland Moodie's representations of racial difference, and their writing also reveals varying degrees of awareness of their own enmeshment in colonial practices that entailed the displacement and exploitation of Indigenous peoples. Some of these internal inconsistencies might be attributed to the "ad hoc" and piecemeal quality of migrant writing. But they also confirm that Romantic-era opposition to slavery was compatible with racism.

Slave narratives and migrant narratives are centripetal genres. That is, they are generally addressed from the outskirts of empire to a metropolitan reading public. Prince was aware that Pringle's support would enable her to reach this public and decided to publish her story so "that good people in England might hear from a slave what a slave had felt and suffered" (Prince, 2000, p. 3). We have no access to an unmediated account of Prince's experiences as an enslaved person because she and Pringle sought to render those experiences legible to a white metropolitan English readership. Pringle explains in his Preface to the *History* that Strickland recorded the narrative as it came from Prince's "own lips," and that he "afterwards pruned into its present shape, retaining, as far as was practicable, Mary's exact expressions and peculiar phraseology" (p. 3). But to appeal to a white, metropolitan, and largely female readership, Prince's account not only had to be "pruned" and stripped of what Pringle calls "prolixities" (p. 3); details about Prince's sexual history also needed to be omitted to protect the delicate sensibilities of Englishwomen. Her sexual abuse by Mr. D–is only hinted at, and Captain Abbot, with whom she had a seven-year relationship, is mentioned only in passing as a gentleman who "lent me some help" when Prince tried to purchase her freedom from Mr. Wood (p. 27). White women were unwilling to extend their sympathies to an enslaved woman they considered sexually impure, failing to realize that enslaved people had as little sexual autonomy as they had economic or political autonomy. As Sandra Pouchet Paquet observes, the *History* was produced "in full self-consciousness of print capitalism as a way of winning English hearts and minds in the struggle to abolish slavery" (2002, p. 38). Published just as Parliament was debating the choice between immediate and gradual emancipation of slaves in Britain's colonies, Prince's story offered abolitionists a valuable opportunity not only to illustrate in graphic terms the horrors of slavery but also to emphasize the cruelties of the contingent or partial freedom that enslaved persons were granted while resident in Britain.

Migrant narratives too were written for a metropolitan readership, but their claims on that readership were different and much less urgent than Prince's. In describing unfamiliar landscapes and peoples, and in recounting the challenges and triumphs of settlement to British readers, their authors implicitly staked a claim to belong culturally to the metropolitan center, despite their geographical distance from it. If London was, in Joseph Rezek's words, "the cultural capital of the Anglophone Atlantic," settlers and sojourners often found themselves living at a distance even from "provincial literary centers" such as Philadelphia, New York, Edinburgh, and Dublin (2015, pp. 3, 4). Their experiences undermine a simple opposition between metropole and province, or imperial center and peripheries, reminding us that in the early nineteenth century, locations such as Cape Town, Toronto, or Kingston might be provincial compared to London but metropolitan in relation to the Baviaans River valley, the Canadian backwoods, or a Grenada plantation. British emigrants often settled in places where there was nothing that could be called print culture or a literary marketplace – no booksellers, libraries, or publishing infrastructure. In these cases, their options were to participate in developing a local literary culture or to write for a metropolitan English readership. Frequently, they did both, revising and repurposing their writing for multiple publications and audiences. The pressures of migration required writers to approach authorship pragmatically rather than as a hallowed calling, and as a result, their works are accretive and heterogeneous rather than aesthetically unified entities.

Following the lead of Elizabeth L. Eisenstein and Roger Chartier, historians have tended to assume that print culture was centrifugal, transmitting the values and tastes of metropolitan society outward to the provinces and imperial peripheries. But the many roles print culture played in British imperial expansion require further study. Tony Ballantyne (2007) and Robert Fraser (2008) have challenged the Eurocentric perspective implicit in histories of print. Ballantyne reminds us that "in studying the history of the book in colonized societies – whether settler colonies, plantation colonies, military-garrison colonies, or zones of informal imperialism – we cannot simply transplant European models in an unproblematic manner to the colonized world" (2007, p. 351). Fraser pushes this point farther, observing that the very term "history of the book" implies a Eurocentric orientation and may be of little use in understanding the interactions between colonial and Indigenous literary cultures. Even when colonial societies tried to emulate the practices and standards of the metropolitan literary marketplace, their print cultures were, as Patrick Collier and James T. Conolly observe, "marked by local conditions, affiliations, institutions, and patterns of sociability" (2016, p. 7). The diversity of these local conditions makes it difficult, if not impossible, to provide a general account of colonial print culture or of the interactions between metropolitan and local literary marketplaces. Collier and Conolly thus endorse the value of literary historical case studies, which serve to question and revise narratives of the history of print "that otherwise tend to calcify and become hegemonic" (p. 12). The case study I present here not only offers a new context for understanding the literary impact of Mary Prince's *History*, but also illustrates the interpenetration of metropolitan and settler colonial print culture during the Romantic era, focusing on the examples of South Africa, Upper Canada, and the British West Indies.

1.1 Biographical Details

While the ensuing sections mention biographical details in passing, this section summarizes what we know about the major figures in this study: Prince, her collaborators Pringle and Strickland Moodie, and her antagonist MacQueen. It is intended for those who are not already familiar with these writers or who may not have read *The History of Mary Prince*.

Mary Prince was born into slavery in Brackish Pond, Bermuda in 1788. With her mother and siblings, she was enslaved by Captain and Mrs. Williams, who regarded her as a "pet" for their young daughter (Prince, 2000, p. 7). From this comparatively happy beginning Prince endured a series of sales that tore her from her family and made her the property of an increasingly brutal series of enslavers, from Captain I–'s household at Spanish Point, where she learned "to know the exact difference between the smart of the rope, the cart-whip, and the cow-skin, when applied to [her] naked body" (p. 14); to Mr. D–'s estate on Turks Island, where long days spent working in the salt ponds left her legs "full of dreadful boils, which eat down in some cases to the very bone" (p. 19); and finally to the Woods in Antigua, where she "soon fell ill of the rheumatism" and was left, almost crippled by pain, to recover alone (p. 25). In Antigua, Prince began attending the Moravian Church, and in 1826, she married fellow church-goer Daniel James, a formerly enslaved person who had purchased his freedom. During Prince's enslavement by the Woods, she suffered physical and psychological abuse, relating that although Mrs. Wood "was always finding fault with me, she would not part with me," even when Prince found the means to purchase her freedom (p. 30).

Prince accompanied the Woods to England in 1828 in the hope that a change of climate might alleviate her rheumatism and under the belief that the Woods would grant her freedom there. Once in England, Prince was indeed legally free so long as she remained in the country. But because the Woods would not allow Prince to purchase her freedom, she could not return to Antigua and her husband without also returning to slavery. For several months she continued to endure the Woods' gaslighting, as they alternately "threatened to turn [her] out" of their house and refused to sell Prince her freedom (Prince, 2000, p. 33). Constant abuse eventually drove Prince from the Woods' household even though she "did not know where to go, or how to get [her] living" (p. 33). She initially sought help from the Moravians, whose church she had joined in Antigua, and was subsequently introduced to the Anti-Slavery Society, the members of which provided some "warm clothing and money" until Prince found work as a charwoman (p. 36). In 1829, she "went into the service of Mr and Mrs Pringle," where she found herself "as comfortable as I can be while separated from my dear husband, and away from my own country and all old friends and connections" (p. 36).

Although Prince's narrative ends with her employment by the Pringles, leaving her in a kind of exilic limbo, her trials continued, quite literally. The *History*, which Prince dictated to Susanna Strickland while she was visiting the Pringles, ran through three editions in 1831. It also motivated the enraged John Wood to bring a lawsuit against Pringle for damaging his reputation. When Prince took the witness stand, she acknowledged that she had lived with Captain Abbot for seven years before her marriage to Daniel James, a fact that she had mentioned to Strickland but that had been omitted from the *History*. Prince's courtroom evidence reveals what Salih describes as the "instability" of the *History* (2000, p. xxx), the extent to which it had been shaped to appeal to its audience. The effects of her testimony also reveal *why* this "pruning" was necessary. Not only did Wood win his case for libel, but, after the trial, Prince disappears entirely from the historical record, as if she were no longer of interest or use to the antislavery cause once her sexual history had come to light. Prince is not mentioned in Pringle's or Strickland Moodie's correspondence and her *History* was not republished until 1987. Perhaps she made her way back to Antigua and her husband after the abolition of colonial slavery in 1834. More likely she died friendless and in poverty in London.

Thomas Pringle brought a good deal of experience as a writer and an opponent of slavery to *The History of Mary Prince*. Born into a farming family near the Scottish borders in 1789, Pringle sought admission as a young man to Romantic Edinburgh's literary elite through the portals of periodicals including *Blackwood's Edinburgh Magazine* and the *Scots Magazine*. Although he was found wanting by the Tory writers associated with *Blackwood's*, Pringle found a patron in Walter Scott, who sponsored his emigration to the Cape of Good Hope, which had become a British possession in 1814. Emigration offered Pringle the prospect of reconciling his family's farming heritage with his own literary endeavors. In 1812, Pringle's father had lost the lease on the land his ancestors had farmed for more than a century, and the family's financial difficulties were exacerbated by the economic depression that affected many tenant farmers in the wake of the Napoleonic Wars (Devine, 2011, p. 125). Pringle emigrated to the South African Cape with his wife, father, and other members of his family in 1819 as part of a government-funded scheme. They were allocated land at the eastern frontier, near the Neutral or Ceded Territory from which the British had recently driven Indigenous peoples including the Xhosa and San. By his own account, Pringle had two objects in participating in the emigration scheme: "to collect again into one social circle, and establish in rural independence, my father's family," and, setting aside his literary ambitions for the moment, "to obtain, through the recommendation of powerful friends, some moderate appointment, suitable to my qualifications, in the civil service of the colony" (1834, p. 119).

Two years later, a position at the South African Public Library enabled Pringle to move to Cape Town, where, with his friend John Fairbarn, he quickly established a monthly journal, a weekly newspaper, a school for the sons of English settlers, and a literary and scientific society. Pringle's efforts to promote literary culture, and with it the kind of free critical inquiry that might challenge the colonial administration's treatment of South African Indigenous peoples, incurred the wrath of the colony's governor, Lord Charles Somerset, who implemented what Pringle described as "the Cape 'Reign of Terror'" – a "frightful system of espionage" intended "to strike down every man who should dare even to look or think disapprobation" of the colonial government (1834, pp. 323, 333). Retreating from Cape Town to the interior, Pringle wrote most of the poems that would later be published as *Ephemerides* (1828) before he raised the money needed for his return passage to London. An essay on slavery at the Cape that Pringle wrote before his departure and that was published in Thomas Campbell's *New Monthly Magazine* in 1826 won the attention of the London Anti-Slavery Society, of which Pringle became secretary in 1828. It was during this time that Pringle met Mary Prince and Susanna Strickland. His work as editor for two antislavery journals and a literary annual, and as ghostwriter of two books about South Africa, prevented him from publishing his own long-planned *Narrative of a Residence in South Africa* until 1834. Although conceived of several years before his involvement in the publication of *The History of Mary Prince*, Pringle's *Narrative* reveals his familiarity with the conventions of the slave narrative and suggests the impact Prince had on his work. Pringle intended to return to the Cape shortly after the publication of his *Narrative*, but died from tuberculosis only days before his planned departure (Vigne, 2012).

Susanna Strickland, Prince's amanuensis, represented the primary readership of the *History* – white, middle-class Englishwomen. The postwar recession that sent the Pringles to South Africa ousted Susanna Strickland's family from what John Thurston describes as "their precarious perch among the gentry," which they had occupied only since 1808, when her father, a shipping agent, purchased Reydon Hall in Suffolk (1996, p. 13). Thomas Strickland's death in 1818 left the six Strickland sisters unprovided for, and five of them began writing to support themselves. Susanna Strickland published her first story at the age of nineteen and soon established herself as a writer of sketches, tales, and poems for *La Belle Assemblée*, a fashionable ladies' magazine. But her conversion from Anglicanism to Methodism when she was in her mid-twenties alienated her from her family and led her to question her vocation as a writer.

Under Pringle's guidance, Strickland found in the antislavery movement a focus for her newfound religious zeal and reformed authorial aspirations that bolstered her claims to feminine piety and propriety. It was while she was visiting the man she described as "my dear adopted father, Mr. Pringle" that Strickland took down the narratives of Mary Prince and Ashton Warner, another enslaved person who had sought freedom in England (Ballstadt, Hopkins, and Peterman, 1985, p. 50). In Pringle's home, Strickland also met John Wedderburn Dunbar Moodie, whom she married in 1831. The Moodie family had lost their ancestral estate on Hoy, an island in the Orkneys, and had emigrated to South Africa in 1817 in the hope of repairing their fortunes. John Moodie, owner of a flourishing farm at the Cape, had returned to Britain in 1830 with two aims – to publish a book about South Africa and to find a wife. His courtship of Strickland was tumultuous: he felt he could not afford to raise a family in England and stipulated that emigration must be a condition of their marriage, and she declared in a letter to her friends James and Emma Bird that her "heart would fail" if she was forced to leave England (p. 42).

Nonetheless, Strickland threw in her lot with Moodie, and in September 1832, the couple set out for Upper Canada, where Susanna's brother, Samuel Strickland, had settled in 1825 and where her sister Catherine, who had married Moodie's friend and fellow Orkneyman Thomas Traill, would soon follow them. Samuel Strickland had developed his own literary connections working for the Canada Company under the superintendence of novelist John Galt and alongside William Dunlop, author of *Statistical Sketches of Upper Canada, for use by emigrants* (1832). Strickland would publish his own account of settler life, *Twenty-Seven Years in Canada West*, in 1853. Catherine Parr Traill, who had distinguished herself as a writer of stories for children before emigrating, published *The Backwoods of Canada; being letters from the wife of an emigrant officer, illustrative of the domestic economy of British America* in 1836. Despite the proximity of these family members, Susanna Strickland Moodie only reluctantly came to consider Canada home, and she never ceased to lament leaving England. One of the aspects of life in the backwoods that she most deplored was her distance from centers of literary culture. She wrote much of her best-known work, *Roughing It in the Bush* (1852), during the 1830s while enduring the poverty and isolation this narrative describes. In the wake of the Upper Canada Rebellion of 1837, when the Moodies removed from the back-woods to the town of Belleville, she began to publish parts of what would eventually become *Roughing It* in the Toronto-based *Literary Garland* and her own short-lived *Victoria Magazine*. Twenty years after the Moodies emigrated, *Roughing It* was finally published by Richard Bentley in London. *Roughing It* reveals the impact of Prince's *History* in its formal features, but although Strickland Moodie wrote extensively and sometimes sympathetically about Canada's Indigenous peoples, she seemed to have left her abolitionist fervor behind her when she emigrated.

The last of the key figures in this study, James MacQueen, was in many senses Pringle's proslavery counterpart, a well-connected editor and writer who brought eyewitness accounts of colonial slavery to metropolitan readers. He occupied "a central place" in a proslavery network developed "through corres-pondence and publication, [and] through the traffic in commodities and wealth" (Lambert, 2008, p. 406). I include him here not because his writing was influenced by Prince's *History* – although he certainly reacted strongly against it – but because Prince's *History* played an important role in disturbing this proslavery network, and through MacQueen's opposition, gained wider notice in the West Indies than it might have done had proslavery writers simply ignored it. Born in Lanarkshire in 1778, MacQueen was one of approximately seventeen thousand Scots who emigrated to the Caribbean in the second half of the eighteenth century (Hamilton, 2005, pp. 23–24). Like many of these emigrants, MacQueen was a sojourner rather than a permanent settler, using his time as overseer at the Westerhall estate in Grenada to make money and forge political connections before returning to Scotland. MacQueen drew on his experiences as an overseer in his aggressively proslavery books *The West India Colonies* (1824) and *The Colonial Controversy* (1825), which won him the editorship of the strongly Tory and proslavery *Glasgow Courier*. MacQueen's inflammatory remarks about the *History* in the pages of *Blackwood's Edinburgh Magazine* compelled Pringle to bring a libel suit against the magazine's London publisher, Thomas Cadell, which in turn elicited a retaliatory lawsuit from Prince's former owner John Wood. Prince's testimony at these trials constitutes her last appearance in the historical record (Thomas, 2005). MacQueen, by contrast, lived until 1870, winning accolades for his work on the geography of Africa.

1.2 Organization

This study is divided into three sections, the first of which focuses on genre. Section 2 discusses the conventions of the slave narrative displayed in *The History of Mary Prince* and examines how the migrant narratives that Pringle and Strickland Moodie went on to write incorporated these conventions. Prince's *History* displays formal features that are common to other early slave narratives: it is built through accretion, repetition, and the incorporation of multiple voices and documents. But it diverges importantly from previous narratives in taking the home rather than the ship as its chronotope – the overriding image that provides a focal point for the complexities of the enslaved person's experiences. The homesickness that permeates Prince's narrative raised the ire of her enslavers and their proslavery supporters, who denied enslaved people the right to cultivate place-based social and familial bonds. Subsequent female-authored slave narratives and migrant narratives both followed Prince in adopting the home as a chronotope. Comparing Strickland Moodie's expressions of homesickness to Prince's demonstrates the extent to which both the home and homesickness were racialized and gendered constructs ordinarily reserved for white women.

Section 3 focuses on print culture, examining how Prince, Pringle, and Strickland Moodie, along with proslavery author James MacQueen, sought to establish their authority in the metropolitan literary marketplace, and how race, gender, and migration shaped their access to print. It describes how Pringle and MacQueen, as migrant writers, mediated the representations of slavery that circulated between colonial and metropolitan print cultures. Their experiences of censorship and political partisanship in South Africa and the West Indies, respectively, informed their participation in metropolitan debates over the "truth" of colonial slavery. This section also examines how Susanna Strickland Moodie's position as a metropolitan reader and writer shaped the publication of Prince's *History*. The first-person testimony of enslaved people converted Strickland Moodie to the antislavery cause and inspired her belief in the potential of print to initiate social reform. Although Prince's *History* arguably did help to bring about the abolition of slavery in Britain's colonies, it did so at the cost of suppressing her voice.

Section 4 situates the publication of *The History of Mary Prince* in the broader context of Pringle's and Strickland Moodie's writing, focusing on their explorations of the relationship between British migration and settlement, and the displacement and exploitation of Black and Indigenous peoples. Pringle became aware of the impact of settler colonialism on Black and Indigenous peoples during his six years in South Africa, well before he met Mary Prince. Although he acknowledged the causal relationship between the clearance of cotters from their land in Scotland and the displacement of Indigenous peoples from their land in South Africa, he remained committed to an ideal of benevolent Christian colonialism that he believed would gradually transform rather than quickly destroy Indigenous ways of life. Strickland Moodie's writing reveals the influence of her collaboration with Prince and Pringle both in her representations of the consequences of British emigration for Black and Indigenous peoples and in her search for providential meaning in her experiences as a migrant. Yet the time she spent as Prince's amanuensis seems to have faded quickly into an idealized fantasy of her past in England. A brief conclusion, presented in Section 5, examines the literary afterlives of Prince, Strickland Moodie, and Pringle, showing how their writings have continued to fascinate writers whose own lives and works sustain and investigate the legacies of settler colonialism, dispossession, and enslavement.

The story map originally accompanying this text aims to situate the publication of the *History* in the context of developments in provincial and metropolitan print cultures throughout the Black and Anglophone Atlantic worlds.[3] It encourages us to consider how access to print culture was delimited by geography, and how the uneven development of print culture throughout the

---

[3] The map's URL is https://arcg.is/08zKay.

Anglophone Atlantic in turn shaped attitudes toward slavery and racial difference. Users can click on vector points on the map to learn more about the development of print culture in Britain, Upper Canada, South Africa, and the West Indies, some details of which are discussed in Section 2. They can also click on the dates in the biographical timelines to locate key events in the lives of Prince, Pringle, Strickland Moodie, and MacQueen.

2 From Slave Narrative to Migrant Narrative

This section explains the conventions of slave narratives before examining how those conventions may have made their way into migrant narratives through *The History of Mary Prince*. Pringle's and Strickland Moodie's migrant narratives share many of the formal features found in the *History*: they are multiauthored, collaborative texts that assert the truth of their representations through repetition, multivocality, and the incorporation of legitimating documents. Slave narratives and migrant narratives thus challenge the Romantic ideals of authorship as an autonomous act of original genius and the literary work as an organically unified aesthetic entity.

While Prince's narrative displays many of the formal features found in other early slave narratives, it also made an important innovation in taking the home as its focal point. Home, for Prince, was not just a domestic space – a room or a dwelling – of her own. It was a concept that also encompassed familial and place-based social bonds. Her assertion of her right to a home and her right to feel homesickness angered her proslavery opponents because, as Strickland Moodie's *Roughing It* illustrates vividly, home and homesickness were gendered and racialized constructs belonging to white women. Reading Strickland's narrative against Prince's illuminates the radical import of the latter's expressions of homesickness.

2.1 Formal Features

Nicole Aljoe has demonstrated the diversity and fluidity of early slave narratives, which she defines as those published before 1845, when the extreme popularity of *Narrative of the Life of Frederick Douglass, An American Slave, Written by Himself* made it a model for subsequent authors to imitate (2014, pp. 4–5). Nonetheless, these early narratives do tend to share a few basic features. For a start, most were dictated to a white European amanuensis, and *The History of Mary Prince* is no exception. Susanna Strickland recorded Prince's story as it came from Prince's "own lips," including all of "the narrator's repetitions and prolixities" (Prince, 2000, p. 3). The transcription was then edited by Thomas Pringle, who claimed to retain "as far as was practicable, Mary's exact expressions and peculiar phraseology" (p. 3). Pringle assures readers that the published account is "essentially her own," and that any changes he had made were simply "to render it clearly intelligible" (p. 3). The cultural insensitivity of Pringle's editing has understandably frustrated scholars, who point out that what Pringle perceived as ungrammatical or redundant may have been perfectly acceptable phrasing in the Creole English that Prince would have spoken (Baumgartner, 2001, pp. 261–264; Allen, 2012, pp. 510–514). But the editing of Prince's text was hardly unusual. Ryan Hanley observes that Black authors were much more likely than their white counterparts "to depend on networks – of friends, co-religionists, conspirators, and even those we might think of as their enemies – for publication, financial support or social prestige" (2019, p. 2). One of the costs these networks exacted was a loss of narrative control, as Black-authored texts "underwent more direct forms of outside influence before publication – i.e. edition, transcription and censorship" (p. 8). Our access to the enslaved person's voice is thus irrevocably mediated.

Even so, the central feature of a slave narrative, according to Robert Stepto, is the enslaved person's voice, "recounting, exposing, appealing, apostrophizing, and above all *remembering* his ordeal in bondage" (1991, p. 3). Yet, Stepto adds, "slave narratives are full of other voices, which ... may belong to other 'characters' in the 'story,' but mainly ... appear in the other documents written by slaveholders and abolitionists alike" (p. 256). Again, Prince's narrative is exemplary in this respect. From the opening "I," her voice holds the narrative together. But she includes within it the voices and stories of other enslaved people, such as Henry the Black slave driver, "who confessed that he had treated the slaves very cruelly; but said that he was compelled to obey the orders of his master" (Prince, 2000, p. 28); and Hetty, whose kindness and whose cries – "Massa! Have mercy upon me – don't kill me outright" (p. 14) – Prince cannot forget. The voices of other enslaved people serve to amplify Prince's own and demonstrate that her experiences were not unique. Hetty's sufferings under the violence of a brutal enslaver prefigure Prince's, and Henry's utter lack of moral autonomy reflects Prince's sense of shame when she is forced against her will to bathe the "indecent" Mr. D– (p. 24). Prince's narrative also occasionally includes the voices of her enslavers, which allows her to contest their construction of her identity by rendering it subservient to her own representation. Thus, when Prince reports that Mrs. Wood "called me a black devil" (p. 31), the epithet becomes proof of Mrs. Wood's cruelty and hypocrisy in refusing to let Prince purchase her freedom rather than of Prince's ill nature, as Mrs. Wood intended it.

As Stepto observes, the other voices that feature in slave narratives often appear as paratext, adjacent to the narrative itself. The function of this paratext is usually to legitimate the narrative by serving as a testament to its veracity or providing context for understanding it. For instance, Harriet Jacobs's *Incidents in the Life of a Slave Girl* (1861) was prefaced by an introduction from American novelist and abolitionist Lydia Maria Child testifying to her "confidence" in the "veracity" of Jacobs's account of the abuse she suffered in slavery and the amazing circumstances of her eventual escape to the North (Jacobs, 2019, p. 6). Child, who edited *Incidents* for publication, reassured readers that "both the ideas and the language" of the story belonged to Jacobs (p. 6). In words that echo Pringle's, Child explained that as editor she had simply "pruned excrescences a little" (p. 6). The practice of legitimating Black-authored texts with white-authored paratext was not confined to slave narratives. For instance, the poems of Phillis Wheatley were prefaced by a document signed by public figures, including the governor and lieutenant governor of Massachusetts, testifying that Wheatley was indeed their author. Pringle's preface to Prince's *History* performs a similar authenticating function, assuring readers that "no fact of importance has been omitted, and not a single circumstance or sentiment has been added" (Prince, 2000, p. 3). Yet Pringle's preface also acknowledges Prince's agency in initiating the publication of her narrative. He begins by establishing that "the idea of writing Mary Prince's history was first suggested by herself. She wished it to be done, she said, that good people in England might hear from a slave what a slave had felt and suffered" (p. 3). Prince's aim here is consistent with other slave narratives. In addition to allowing the author to write herself "into being," as Sterling Bland has suggested (1990, p. 4), slave narratives tended to be pedagogical in intent, aiming to teach a white European readership about the brutalities of slavery.

Prince's narrative was not only prefaced by Pringle, but also postfaced by him in a long supplement that incorporated several letters from Prince's enslaver John Wood attacking Prince's character and from others defending it. The editor's supplement effectively takes the form of a court hearing. Pringle first performs a rhetorical cross-examination of Wood, pointing out the logical fallacy in Wood's refusal to allow Prince to buy her freedom because she is allegedly "an abandoned and worthless woman" but nonetheless allowing this depraved character to care for his child (Prince, 2000, p. 41). He then introduces his own "evidence," letters from Joseph Phillips, a merchant in Antigua, and Mrs. Forsyth, who employed Prince in the summer of 1829, after she had left the Woods' household (p. 49). These letters serve as character witnesses for Prince, with Phillips calling into question Wood's slanderous representation of Prince's conduct in Antigua, and Forsyth attesting to Prince's "excellent character" while in her employment (p. 54). Pringle's analyses of these documents are followed by two appendices that offer additional forms of testimony. A letter to the Birmingham Ladies' Society for Relief of Negro Slaves signed by four women, including Susanna Strickland and Pringle's wife, certifies that Prince's back is "distinctly scarred, and, as it were, *chequered*, with vestiges of severe floggings" (p. 64). As Barbara Baumgartner (2001) has argued, Prince's body here becomes evidence for the truth of her narrative, but, again, it must be interpreted and legitimated by white intermediaries. Following the letter, the short "Narrative of Louis Asa-Asa, a Captured African" concludes *The History of Mary Prince*.

One of the effects of this compilation of documents is repetition, as these documents invite us to approach Prince's story from a variety of perspectives. Jessica Allen (2012) and Rachel Banner (2013) have examined the function of repetition at the semantic level in Prince's narrative, suggesting that as a literary device it both creates a sense of enslavement as an experience of endlessly reiterated horrors and emphasizes the narrative's "status as a constructed artifact and Mary Prince's corresponding status as artist/author on the same level as the *History*'s paratextual interlocutors" (Banner, 2013, p. 306). At the structural level, repetition in Prince's *History* also serves to affirm the truth of her account of slavery and the representativeness of her experiences. For instance, "The Narrative of Louis Asa-Asa," which is appended to Prince's narrative, confirms that her liminal status in England, nominally free but only as long as she did not return home, was not unique. A native of West Africa, Asa-Asa was captured and "sold six times over" by slave traders but was freed when weather forced the French ship carrying him to dock in St Ives, Cornwall (Prince, 2000, p. 67). Although relieved to be once more free, Asa-Asa acknowledges the loneliness of his situation: "I am very happy to be in England, as far as I am very well;–but I have no friend belonging to me, but God, who will take care of me as he has done already" (p. 69). Like Prince, Asa-Asa is separated from family and community and must choose between returning to them and the possibility of recapture and re-enslavement or remaining alone in England. Echoing Prince, Asa-Asa concludes, "I should like much to see my friends again, but I do not now wish to go back to them: for if I go back to my own country, I might be taken as a slave again. I would rather stay here, where I am free, than go back to my country to be sold" (p. 69).

Some readers have dismissed Asa-Asa's narrative as a symptom of Pringle's "excessive" intervention in the text, seeing it as "unrelated to Mary Prince's" story (Baumgartner, 2001, p. 261).[4] But it is precisely because of the similarities in Prince's and Asa-Asa's situation in England that Pringle included it. Repetition makes a point. In his editorial supplement to Prince's narrative,

---

[4] See also Rauwerda, 2001, p. 399.

Pringle deplores the limbo in which Prince and Asa-Asa have been left, arguing that England cannot rightly be called a free country "when the slave landed in England still only possesses that qualified degree of freedom that a change of domicile will determine it" and urging "the present Government to introduce a Bill into the Legislature making perpetual that freedom which the slave has acquired by his passage here" (Prince, 2000, p. 63). The documents of which *The History of Mary Prince* is comprised constitute variations on a theme, harmonizing to assert the truth of Prince's depiction of slavery and to call into question the claims of her detractors.

Romantic-era migrant narratives share many of the formal features of slave narratives. Pringle's and Strickland Moodie's migrant narratives, relatively early instances of this quintessentially nineteenth-century genre, may have been shaped by their work on *The History of Mary Prince*. Like slave narratives, migrant narratives tend to be built through accretion, repetition, and the incorporation of multiple voices and documents. And these formal features serve a similar function in both genres – to attest to the truth of experiences that are foreign to readers. On one hand, tracing the similarities between the formal features of slave narratives and migrant narratives allows us to see them as belonging to a common literary culture that has been overlooked in the study of Romantic literature, one that understands authorship as a pragmatic rather than as a hallowed calling and literary works as malleable, collaborative, and heterogeneous rather than organic, unified, and integral. But on the other hand, exploring these structural similarities also serves to illuminate the vast differences in power and agency between enslaved people and free migrants.

One of the most obvious similarities between slave narratives and migrant narratives is their incorporation of multiple voices and documents in ways that undermine the Romantic ideal of the author as autonomous creator and solitary genius. Pringle had experience in shaping other writers' narratives before he took his pruning shears to Prince's. On his return from Cape Town, Pringle deferred work on what would become the *Narrative of a Residence in South Africa* (1834) in order to collaborate on two other writers' narratives. In an instance of what we might now call ghostwriting, he transformed the notes of his friend George Thompson into *Travels and Adventures in Southern Africa* (1827), incorporating seven of his own previously published poems in the text, but making no overt mention of his hand in writing the book. Pringle also "contributed considerably, and anonymously," to Catherine Richardson's *Scenes and Occurrences in Albany and Cafferland* (1827) (Vigne, 2012, p. 140). Pringle likely was paid for his work on these narratives, and money, given the outstanding debts he had accrued at Cape Town, was more valuable than any fame his own work might have brought him. His unattributed hand in fashioning these narratives is arguably on a continuum with his "pruning" of Mary Prince's narrative. However, Pringle's decision to make known his interventions in Prince's text, but not in Thompson's or Richardson's, indicates the important difference – that a Black woman's narrative needed to be visibly underwritten by a white man's authority, while Thompson's and Richardson's did not.

Pringle's own *Narrative of a Residence in South Africa* lacks the unifying voice that we would expect from a single-authored narrative. When, in 1833, Pringle finally began to work in earnest on the book about South Africa that he had been planning to write since 1820, all his prior writings on the topic proved useful. As Pringle's final work, it effectively constituted a curated compilation of his previous writings about the Cape, or, as he explained in a letter to his friend John Fairbarn, of "all my old scraps worth collecting" (Vigne, 2011, p. 359). These "scraps" included pieces he had written for the *Anti-Slavery Monthly Reporter*, the *Oriental Herald and Colonial Record*, the *Cape Town Gazette*, and *Penny Magazine*. These journals addressed quite disparate readerships ranging from settler colonialists to working-class Britons, and this left the *Narrative* a hodgepodge of tones and styles. The *Narrative* also incorporated letters from Pringle's correspondents, passages from his journal – "exactly as they were written down" (1834, p. 160) – and material that he had contributed to Thompson's and Richardson's books. There is no indication that Pringle's associates or readers considered such "recycling" in any way untoward.

Strickland Moodie's *Roughing It in the Bush* also bears the imprint of collaborative authorship. Although *Roughing It* appeared under Strickland Moodie's name, it represented the work of several hands. Gillian Whitlock aptly proposes that Strickland Moodie "should be conceived as the initiator and focus of a long process of textual activity called *Roughing It in the Bush*, rather than an autonomous author in the conventional sense" (2000, p. 40). *Roughing It* epitomizes the compendiousness, heterogeneity, and instability of migrant narratives. It consists of a series of "simple sketches" and what Strickland Moodie describes as "a few small poems" incorporated to "diversify" the account (2007, p. 11). About two-thirds of the text had been published in North American periodicals before it made its London debut. Of the fifty-five poems it included, only eleven were written specifically for *Roughing It*. Sketch XXIV, "The Whirlwind," begins with a poem by Strickland Moodie's brother, Samuel Strickland, and the sketch itself is drawn from a newspaper article he wrote about "a whirlwind which passed the town of Guelph in the summer of 1829" (p. 292). Several additional poems and four of the sketches were authored by Strickland Moodie's husband, John Wedderburn Dunbar Moodie, whose voice suddenly emerges in "The Village Hotel" and "The Land Jobber" "to afford a connecting link between my wife's sketches, and to account for some circumstances connected with our situation, which otherwise would be unintelligible to the reader" (p. 146). These circumstances concern some misguided investments that accounted for the Moodies' impoverishment during their early years in Canada, and the decision to allow her husband to explain them might reflect either Strickland Moodie's deference on economic matters or her desire to distance herself from his mistakes.

Strickland Moodie's geographical distance from London undermined her authorial control over the shape of *Roughing It*. The book's London publication was a triumph for Strickland Moodie, serving as a metonymic or surrogate return to the country that she never ceased to regret leaving. But publication in London came at a cost, requiring her to renounce some authority over her text. Decisions about which sketches would be included in the book were made by her publisher Richard Bentley and his assistant John Bruce based on what they had at hand when they were ready to go to press, and Bentley seems to have chosen the title for the text that Strickland Moodie called simply "Canadian Life" (Thurston, 1996, p. 137). Within weeks of its British publication, *Roughing It* retraversed the Atlantic, with George Putnam of New York issuing a cheap pirated American edition replete with what Strickland Moodie described as "*Yankee Omissions*" (Ballstadt, 1965, p. 127). Its American editor, Charles Frederick Briggs, explained that he had excised "certain passages of a purely personal or political character, which could have possessed no interest for the American reader," with the aim of transforming it into "a genuine romance, which has all the interest of an imaginative creation" (1852, p. iii). The Putnam edition, in other words, sought to transform *Roughing It* into a novel. John Thurston observes that, as a result of its transatlantic textual history, *Roughing It* is "seriously unstable in its most basic features" (1996, p. 7). Its instability is manifest in "wandering commas, spurs of exclamation, appearing and disappearing majuscules, variant spellings, substitutions, pages lost, found, rearranged, dialogue that is silenced, chapters that fail to make the Atlantic crossing or arrive shuffled, disoriented" (p. 138). There is no consensus as to what an authoritative text of *Roughing It* might look like, as publishers and editors from Bentley onward have revised, excised, and added material, sometimes silently.

In addition to its collaborative production, Prince's *History* also shares with migrant narratives its incorporation of authoritative paratext such as passages from newspaper articles, court records, and correspondence. As I have shown, incorporation of such material into slave narratives served to authenticate accounts that were considered lacking in authority or truth value because of the color of the author's skin. They played a similarly authenticating role in migrant narratives, which may have drawn their use of the device from slave narratives. Emigrants were not perceived by Britons at home as inherently lacking authority, but their narratives did attempt to convey to a metropolitan readership scenes and experiences with which those readers were unfamiliar and that they had no way to verify except by comparison with other accounts. Thus Catherine Parr Traill's *The Backwoods of Canada* (1836) includes excerpts from authoritative sources such as John MacGregor's *British America* (1832) and *Information Published By His Majesty's Commissioners For Emigration, Respecting The British Colonies In North America* (1832). Pringle's *Narrative* incorporates passages from John Barrow's seminal *Travels into the Interior of South Africa* (1806), George Thompson's *Travels and Adventures in South Africa* (1827), and Stephen Kay's *Travels and Researches in Caffraria* (1833), among other influential works. Its voluminous footnotes include entire letters from Pringle to Lord Chancellor Henry Brougham and extensive excerpts from parliamentary papers associated with an official inquiry into the conduct of Lord Charles Somerset, the governor of the Cape during Pringle's residence there.

Slave narratives and migrant narratives incorporated legitimating paratext from authoritative sources because both genres described scenes and experiences that most of their readers would not have experienced firsthand. One of the effects of these narrative supplements is to create consistency through repetition. Honor Rieley (2016) has argued persuasively that such repetition would be reassuring to readers of migrant narratives who were themselves considering emigration and who might be troubled by conflicting accounts of colonial settlement. Traill's *Backwoods of Canada* consists of letters she originally wrote to friends and relatives in England, and the content of a letter to one recipient is often repeated in a letter to another. Letter XI, addressed to a "dear friend," reiterates in condensed form much of the detail of Letters I through VII, all of which are addressed to Traill's mother. This might suggest that Traill did little editing of the work as a whole, instead conceiving of each letter as a discrete text. However, Rieley's research suggests it is also possible that Traill did not regard repetition as something that she needed to eliminate from her text, but rather as something that added to its truth value.

While Pringle's and Moodie's behind-the-scenes pruning of Prince's narrative looks to twenty-first-century readers like unwarranted and condescending interference, it was on a continuum with their practices in other texts and contexts. From ghostwriting to compiling and publishing work by multiple hands under a single author's name or republishing versions of the same story under several different titles, the authorial practices of migrant writers challenge our post-Romantic respect for the integrity of the literary work and the autonomy of the author. The pressures of migration – economic hardship, daily bodily labor, lack of basic resources – required writers to approach authorship pragmatically rather than as a hallowed calling and to understand their work as accretive and heterogeneous rather than organic and unified. Writing, for migrants, was something accomplished in moments of rest after hard physical labor, using scarce and expensive paper and ink, in the knowledge that what was written might never be read.

2.2 Home and Homesickness

Although Prince's *History* shares many of the formal features of early slave narratives, it was arguably as seminal for female-authored slave narratives as Frederick Douglass's was for male-authored versions of the genre because it offered a new and gendered chronotope. Paul Gilroy identified the ship as the chronotope of the slave narrative – the cultural configuration that captures the distinctive concerns of the genre. The ship, "a living micro-cultural, micro-political system in motion," represents the circulation of people, ideas, and material objects throughout the Black Atlantic (Gilroy, 1995, p. 4). Following Gilroy, scholars such as Vincent Caretta (2003) have emphasized the extraordinary mobility of enslaved people, going so far as to ally the slave narrative with the travel narrative. As the story map illustrates, Prince covered about seven thousand miles in oceanic crossings during her lifetime (Gadpaille, 2016, p. 65), yet I would argue that rather than taking the ship as its chronotope, the *History* takes the home, a space associated with nineteenth-century ideals of white feminine chastity and domesticity. In doing so, it not only prefigures later nineteenth-century slave narratives by women, such as Harriet Jacobs's *Incidents in the Life of a Slave Girl*, but it also set the tone for migrant narratives, which similarly take the home as their chronotope. Home, as an absent presence, is at the center of Prince's slave narrative and of the migrant narratives it influenced.

Because she was an enslaved woman, Prince's relationship to white, middle-class notions of domesticity was complicated. Jenny Sharpe explains that enslaved women "existed outside the structures of domesticity but had to uphold its ideals" in order to be found worthy of freedom by white middle-class Britons (2002, p. 121). And Charlotte Sussman similarly observes that antislavery advocates attempted to situate slave women within "the categories of English domesticity" in order to make them "accessible to abolitionist sentiments," but at the expense of erasing the particularities of their experiences (2000, p. 130). In Prince's case, this meant omitting her sexual relationships from her narrative; although Prince had "no self-autonomy as a slave, she was expected to exercise a sexual autonomy over her body" (Sharpe, 2002, p. 121). Pringle's aim in obscuring Prince's sexual history was undoubtedly, as Sara Salih suggests, "to spare the prudish sensibilities of potential readers" who might be unwilling to extend their sympathy to a woman their standards would deem impure or "fallen" (2000, p. ix). Sharpe, Baumgartner, and Hanley, among others, have read the *History* against the grain in order to probe its strategic silences surrounding Prince's sexual relationships. This form of reading has the effect of perpetuating its original readers' concern with Prince's sexuality, albeit with the intention of liberating her from the mores imposed upon her by proslavery and antislavery writers alike.

However, it is important to recognize that enslaved women's oblique relation to white, middle-class "structures of domesticity" was not limited to their sexuality, but also included their sense of affective community – something that Prince addresses frequently. For Prince, home is associated primarily with affective community rather than with a particular geographic location or a dwelling place. Elizabeth Bohls notes that Prince frequently "uses the word 'heart' throughout her narrative to invoke a network of affective connections and community values" (2014, p. 176). Prince's account of her successive displacements highlights the emotional impact of the loss of her original famil-ial community and asserts her right to feel homesick at a time when homesick-ness was understood as a disease that belonged particularly to white women. Proslavery responses to the *History*, which stringently deny her attachments to an affective community in Antigua, suggest the novelty of her claim.

Enslaved peoples were deprived of a home – a place associated with security, affection, and autonomy. Moreover, enslaved peoples' movements were dic-tated by their owners, and they were likely to be sold without notice or regard for their preferences or attachments to people and places. Orlando Patterson refers to the resulting phenomenon as "natal alienation," describing enslaved peoples as "genealogical isolate[s]" because they were so entirely cut off from family and heritage (1982, p. 5). The social relationships that enslaved people formed "were never recognized as legitimate and binding" by their enslavers (p. 6). Mary Prince's narrative vividly describes the lived experience of natal alienation as she is repeatedly sold and bought by her enslavers. She recalls her childhood in Brackish Pond, where she was enslaved by Captain and Mrs. Williams, as "the happiest period of my life" (2000, p. 7) because she lived with her mother, who "was a household slave in the same family" (p. 7), and her siblings, who were her "play-fellows and companions" (p. 7). Here Prince was temporarily protected from the "toil and sorrow" that would domin-ate her later years. Prince's recollection of this familial community demon-strates to readers her deep capacity for affection and attachment, a capacity that apologists for slavery often denied to Black people (Ellis, 1996, pp. 127–128). This familial community became increasingly precious to Prince as it grew geographically and temporally distant.

Prince's *History* chronicles a series of moves away from her birthplace and the affective community that it represents. When Mrs. Williams hires her out to Mrs. Pruden, who lives five miles away, Prince "thought my young heart would break, it pained me so" (2000, p. 8). She recalls the "sore trial" of finding herself in "a strange house … among strange people," but retrospectively recognizes the experience as "light, light to the trials I have since endured!" (p. 8). Her removal to this "strange house" is the first of many displacements, perhaps the most traumatic of which is her sale at a slave auction. Almost three decades later, she "cannot bear to think of that day," nor can she find words to convey what she "then felt and suffered" (p. 10). The slave auction inverts the trope of the unfeeling Black perpetuated by supporters of slavery, for while Prince's "heart throbbed with grief and terror," none "of the many by-standers, who were looking at us so carelessly, [thought] of the pain that wrung the hearts of the negro woman and her young ones" (p. 11). The auction dehumanizes Prince and her siblings, as potential buyers treat them like livestock. But perhaps worse than the dehumanization, Prince suggests, are "the bitter pains which follow such separations as these. All that we love taken away from us" (p. 10). After she is sold again, to Captain I–, Prince's "thoughts went back continually to those from whom I had been so suddenly parted" (p. 13). She repeatedly endures the trauma of forced separation from those she loves. When Captain I– sells her to Mr. D–, who takes her to Turks Island, she is "not permitted to see [her] mother or father, or poor sisters and brothers, to say good bye, though [she is] going away to a strange land, and might never see them again" (p. 18). Prince's time on Turks Island is a prolonged exile, during which, she recalls, "my heart yearned to see my native place again, my mother, and my kindred" (p. 22). The trials of her years with Mr. D–, including overwork and sexual abuse, are heightened by separation from those she loves.

After she is sold at auction, Prince must look to her fellow slaves for the affective community her family once provided, and she is unable to create anything approaching her childhood experience in her subsequent situations. In Captain I–'s household at Spanish Point, Prince becomes attached to Hetty, "the most active woman I ever saw," but Hetty's hardships also elicit her horror, as Prince sees what her own future might be like (2000, p. 14). She recalls that Hetty "lived a miserable life, and her death was hastened (at least the slaves all believed and said so) by the dreadful chastisement she received from my master during her pregnancy" (p. 15). The parenthetical aside here gestures toward a community of enslaved people that shares an interpretation of events in the I–

household, one that Prince's "at least" suggests might differ from Captain I–'s account. This community offers a standard of judgment that Prince lacks once she sails for England with the Woods, where her comparative isolation enables Mr. and Mrs. Wood's gaslighting. Nonetheless, this community cannot replace Prince's family, nor are its collective judgments always comforting, as Prince acknowledges when she recollects that "All the slaves said that death was a good thing for poor Hetty, but I cried very much for her death" (p. 16). Prince might recognize some truth in what "all the slaves said," but Hetty's horrific death deprives her of a mother figure and haunts her "mind for many a day" (p. 16). The various slave communities in which Prince finds herself over the course of her *History* are bound together by fear, humiliation, and suffering, as well as by affection. "In telling my own sorrows," she explains, "I cannot pass by those of my fellow-slaves – for when I think of my own griefs, I remember theirs" (p. 22). This remark reminds readers of the *History* that Prince's story is not unique, but it also reminds us that at the moment of telling her story in London, Prince is entirely isolated from her friends and family at home.

Prince's account of her serial displacements provides important context for understanding her plight in England, where she is given the semblance of agency over her movements but must choose between affective community and legal freedom. A few years prior to her journey to England with Mr. and Mrs. Wood, Prince had married Daniel James, a formerly enslaved person who "had purchased his freedom of his mistress" (2000, p. 30). James represents the security and stability Prince has longed for: "He was very industrious after he bought his freedom; and he had hired a comfortable house, and had convenient things about him" (p. 30). Marrying James is an act of self-assertion on Prince's part, a declaration of some degree of autonomy within slavery – of her right to give and receive affection and to have a home of her own. Yet she determines to endure a separation from her husband and accompany the Woods to London because she has been led to believe "that my master would free me" once in England (p. 31). This "false report" leaves Prince with a horrible choice (p. 31). She is legally free in England but cannot return to Antigua and her husband without also returning to slavery – unless Mr. Wood allows her to purchase her freedom. Moreover, the liberty that Prince supposedly enjoys in England is illusory, as the Woods well know. They repeatedly urge her to exercise her freedom by leaving their house, but, as Prince explains, "I knew that I was free in England, but I did not know where to go, or how to get my living" (p. 33). Without friends, money, or employment, and without the means of acquiring any of these, Prince, as Kenneth McNeil has argued, is basically a refugee or asylum seeker – someone who is theoretically free to return to their home

country but for whom return would have severe consequences (2019). To leave
the Woods' household is to embrace poverty, isolation, and uncertainty, and so,
Prince declares, "I should never have gone away had I not been driven out by my
owners" (2000, p. 34).

"To be free is very sweet," Prince repeats several times throughout her
narrative (2000, p. 38). Yet she also expresses repeatedly her longing for
home and family: "My heart yearned to see my native place again, my mother,
and my kindred" (p. 22). So her decision to remain in England, where she is "as
comfortable as I can be while separated from my dear husband, and away from
my own country and all old friends and connections," was by no means an easy
or straightforward one (p. 36). Prince's position at the end of her narrative is
fundamentally unsettled. Having arrived in England as a visitor, she has become
a refugee. As Sandra Pouchet Paquet observes, for Prince, "England is the
means to an end, not the fulfillment of a dream of freedom, as it is in *The
Interesting Life of Olaudah Equiano*" (2002, p. 34). Prince has emphasized
throughout her narrative the importance of affective community, yet she ends
her story severed from her husband, family, and friends. Under these circumstances, nominal freedom can hardly be counted a triumph. Prince continues to
"hope that God will find a way to give me my liberty, *and* give me back to my
husband. I endeavor to keep down my fretting, and to leave all to Him, for he
knows what is good for me better than I know myself. Yet, I must confess, I find
it a hard and heavy task to do so" (2000, p. 37, emphasis added). Prince's
honesty about the difficulty of exercising patience and resigning herself to her
painful circumstances is remarkable given the centrality of conversion to
Christianity in many slave narratives of this period. Like these other slave
narratives, Prince's occasionally represents enslavement as an earthly trial
that will bring religious redemption in an as yet unrevealed providential plan.
It was risky for Prince to acknowledge publicly that she sometimes doubted
God's ultimate goodness and the existence of such a providential plan. But who
in Prince's position would not experience such doubts?

Prince's assertion of her right to a home in the sense of both an autonomous
domestic space and a place-bound affective community was more radical than
scholars have recognized. Kevis Goodman has shown that the concept of
homesickness as a bodily and mental illness emerged in the late eighteenth
century as "a disability of wartime and colonial mobility, a somatic revolt
against forced travel, depopulation, emigration, and other forms of transience"
(2008, p. 196). It is important to clarify that homesickness was a phenomenon
initially recognized among *Europeans* who were displaced by agricultural
enclosure and industrial capitalism in Britain, or who sought to improve their
fortunes in the far reaches of the empire. There was no concern that the

Indigenous peoples these European settlers displaced might also experience homesickness, or that enslaved people, who were also subject to "forced travel," might long for home. Homesickness was not only a white, European condition; by the 1830s, it was also a feminized one. Attachment to home, and consequently a longing for home, was at the moment of Prince's *History* the privilege of white, middle-class women.

Prince's declarations of homesickness raised hackles among those who sought to discredit her. Her enslaver John Wood questioned her attachment to her husband and friends in Antigua, and, implicitly, her motives for wanting to return to them. In a letter written after his return to Antigua, Wood observes rather inconsequentially that Prince "is not a native of this country, and I know of no relation she has here" (Prince, 2000, p. 43). The same, of course, could be said about England, of which Prince similarly was not a native and where she also had no relatives. The *Bermuda Royal Gazette*, which printed a piece in defense of Wood in November 1831, thought it worthwhile to point out that "Mary Prince is not detained from her native land, as evidence[d] from the circumstance of Bermuda and not Antigua being her natal soil." Had Prince returned to Bermuda, she could easily have been re-enslaved, so the point is moot. But the systematic attempt to deny Prince's attachment to her community in Antigua is remarkable, suggesting a general resistance to the idea that slaves, mere property in the eyes of West Indian planters, could experience a sense of belonging. Pringle's refutation of this point in his supplement to Prince's narrative evinces a migrant's understanding of the relativism of home. He asks, "was [Antigua] not her home (so far as a slave can have a home) for thirteen or fourteen years? Were not the connexions, friendships, and associations of her mature life formed there?" (Prince, 2000, p. 46). While Antigua was not Prince's birthplace, she had lived there for longer than any of her previous residences and she exercised what agency she could within the confines of slavery to claim an autonomous domestic space and to cultivate a place-bound affective community.

In taking home rather than a ship as its chronotope, Mary Prince's *History* departed from male-authored slave narratives and set a precedent for female-authored slave narratives. In *Incidents in the Life of a Slave Girl*, Harriet Jacobs repeatedly voices a desire for her own home, a space free from the intrusions of her enslavers where she could care for her children. Like Prince before her, Jacobs understood that sexual purity and domesticity were considered the prerogatives of white women, and that to forfeit the former, even involuntarily, might undermine her right to the latter in the eyes of white readers. Whereas Prince's narrative skirts around the subject of her sexual relationships, both forced and consensual, Jacobs addresses much more directly enslaved women's lack of sexual autonomy through her decision to have an affair with an unmarried white man as a means of evading the sexual advances of her enslaver. This comparative frankness was enabled by Jacobs's decision to publish *Incidents* anonymously and to change the names of everyone mentioned in it, including her own. Admitting that "it seems less degrading to give one's self than to submit to compulsion," Jacobs entreats white women, "whose purity has been sheltered from childhood, who have been free to choose the objects of your affection, whose homes are protected by law, do not judge the poor desolate slave girl too severely" (2019, pp. 49–50). A home "protected by law" is the precondition of the sexual purity so valued by Jacobs's white readers rather than the reward due to pure and virtuous women. Although Jacobs escaped to the North and eventually obtained her freedom, her story lacks the closure that a home would provide: "The dream of my life is not yet realized. I do not sit with my children in a home of my own. I still long for a hearthstone of my own, however humble" (p. 167). Freedom and home in Prince's and Jacobs's narratives are inseparable. One has a home but cannot return to it as a free woman; the other is a free woman but has no home in which to protect and enjoy her liberty.

Home also constitutes the chronotope of Susanna Strickland Moodie's migrant narrative. Like Prince's *History*, Strickland Moodie's narrative is loosely structured through a series of removals from one locale to another, all of which are unsatisfactory stand-ins for the home she has left in England. *Roughing It* is full of the expressions of homesickness that caused such ire among Prince's readers. George Elliott Clarke has remarked parenthetically that, given "Moodie's status as midwife to Prince's *History*, it may be possible to read *Roughing It*, intertextually with Prince, as a displaced 'slave narrative' of a genteel, pioneer English woman, toiling in the bush country of Upper Canada" (2005, p. 13). The very phrasing of this remark, calling attention overtly to Strickland Moodie's class and race, suggests the absurdity of likening her misery to the sufferings of an enslaved person. Strickland Moodie did experience emigration as enforced and involuntary. But her declaration in the introduction to *Roughing It in the Bush* that "in most instances, emigration is a matter of necessity, not of choice" is dramatically undercut by the historical proximity of her own transatlantic passage to the forced migrations of Mary Prince (2007, p. 9). Strickland Moodie had a choice concerning emigration, but it was a choice between what she saw as two distinctly unappealing propositions: remaining in England, where she and her husband would struggle to retain a foothold in the middle class on his half-pay, or emigrating to Canada, where, as they believed, they would thrive as landowners. David Stouck explains that emigration to Canada, in contrast to emigration to the United States, was inherently backward-looking. Britons arrived in Canada "with the modest hope of salvaging a way of life threatened at home" rather than with the aim of pursuing new and better options (1974, p. 471). No wonder that, looking back on her early struggles, Strickland Moodie warns that "emigration may, indeed, generally be regarded as an act of severe duty, performed at the expense of personal enjoyment, and accompanied by the sacrifice of those local attachments which stamp the scenes amid which our childhood grew, in imperishable characters, upon the heart" (2007, p. 9). As it transpired, emigration entailed both the economic hardships and loss of status that Strickland Moodie had hoped to leave behind in England, and the homesickness and trials of emotional endurance that she had anticipated.

Strickland Moodie settled in Canada as part of a community that eventually included her sister Catherine Parr Traill, her brother, Samuel Strickland, and their families. Moreover, she enjoyed her own domestic space, although certainly much inferior to what she had left in England. As a number of scholars have noted, domesticity features importantly in *Roughing It*, reflecting the significance of homemaking in the settler colonial experience (Dean, 1992; Whitlock, 2000, pp. 38–74; Thomas, 2009). Strickland Moodie was aware of the imperative to conform to white, middle-class, metropolitan ideals of femininity, which demanded not only sexual and moral purity but also a degree of leisure to dedicate to refined pursuits and a physical distance from dirty household chores that were impossible to achieve in the backwoods of Canada. Strickland Moodie's rueful recounting of her domestic failures – the inedible bread and the sad little chunk of maple sugar – acknowledges the challenges of keeping the settler colonial household running, let alone achieving the standards of the metropolitan, middle-class household.

Rather than rehearsing again the centrality of home in *Roughing It*, I want to focus here on Strickland Moodie's expressions of homesickness, which find an outlet in her meditations on the natural world. Vivid and at times even melodramatic, these expressions of homesickness reveal the extent to which an attachment to home was the prerogative of white, middle-class women. The Suffolk landscape that Strickland Moodie inhabited before she was a wife, mother, and emigrant features significantly in her expressions of homesickness, perhaps representing for her an escape from the trammels of settler colonial domesticity. She describes this landscape in "Rachel Wilde, or, Trifles from the Burthen of a Life" (1848), a largely autobiographical story. In an instance of the repurposing so common in migrant writing, "Rachel Wilde," which Strickland Moodie first published in installments in *Victoria Magazine*, later became the basis of *Flora Lyndsay* (1854), a lightly fictionalized prequel to *Roughing It* that recounted the decision to emigrate and the voyage to Canada.

"Rachel Wilde" recalls a lived relationship to the Suffolk landscape that Strickland Moodie cannot recreate in Canada. As a child, Rachel feels in good Wordsworthian fashion that she is indeed "wild," a part of the natural world: "The birds were her birds, the trees were her trees, and the flowers were her flowers. She was a queen in the green dominions of nature" (1991, p. 119). Her sense of oneness with nature shades uneasily into a feeling of ownership, an assumption that the natural world exists purely for her enjoyment. Emigration deprives Rachel of this land she had regarded as a possession. The narrator relegates Rachel's "sheer joy" in the prospect of "budding branches" and "white fleecy clouds" to the

> season of youth and innocence – when earth is still the paradise of God, and its crimes and sorrows are veiled from the eyes of the undefiled by the bright Angel of his presence. They see not the flaming sword, they hear not the doom of the exile, but wander hand in hand with pitying spirits through that region of bliss. (p. 119)

Childhood, for Strickland Moodie, is a prelapsarian state, and Adam and Eve's exile from Eden finds a parallel not only in the passage to adulthood, with its awareness of "crimes and sorrows," but also in her passage across the Atlantic, which figures as a punishment for those crimes. Although set prior to Strickland Moodie's "exile," "Rachel Wilde" is permeated with an emigrant's nostalgia for the idealized past of her childhood home. The Suffolk landscape is associated with a sense of mastery and freedom that Strickland Moodie could not replicate in Canada.

Roughing It reveals Strickland Moodie's homesickness through its depictions of the Canadian landscape. With its "ancient forest" and "dark cedar swamp" (2007, p. 178), its fires, whirlwinds, and frozen soil, the Canadian landscape is too threatening and overwhelming to invite a dissolution of the boundaries of the self, let alone a sense of dominion. It is during the passage up the St. Lawrence that Strickland Moodie first feels a sense of estrangement from the Canadian landscape. Gazing at the unfamiliar prospect, she feels "keenly, for the first time … that I was a stranger in a strange land; my heart yearned intensely for my absent home. Home! The word had ceased to belong to my present – it was doomed to live for ever in the past; for what emigrant ever regarded the country of his exile as his home" (p. 32). Indeed, despite her many years' residence in Canada, Strickland Moodie never ceased to regard it as "the country of [her] exile." At times, however, she finds metonymic reminders of home in the Canadian landscape, such as the stream that runs beside the Moodies' first, shed-like dwelling near Cobourg and seems to express "in its deep wailings and fretful sighs" her own "lamenting for the land I had left for ever" (p. 90). Some harebells, the first she has seen in Canada, leave Strickland Moodie overcome by "remembrance of the past" (p. 227). She feels that the flowers "had become holy" because they were "connected with sacred home recollections" (p. 227). Emigration fundamentally changes Strickland Moodie's relationship to the natural world, which becomes above all an antagonist to be tamed into submission and forced to render up its life-sustaining gifts. The harebells momentarily arrest Strickland Moodie not only because they grew at home in England but also because the pleasure she takes in them is aesthetic. Their existence seems purely ornamental, making them a visual luxury in a context where everything is valued according to its use.

Like Prince's *History*, *Roughing It* lacks resolution; it cannot bring its narrator's experiences to a state of closure. *Roughing It* leaves Strickland Moodie in a kind of exilic limbo, ill at ease in the country from which she tells her story yet unable to return to the one she still considers home. Strickland Moodie figures this liminal condition as a kind of living death. Describing the effects of the passage of time on her relationships with her family and friends back in England, she writes, "it is as if the grave had closed over you, and the hearts that once knew and loved you know you no more" (2007, p. 82). The publication in London of *Roughing It*, almost twenty years after she had begun working on it, was a way of speaking from that grave, if not to family members, to the metropolitan literary community of which Strickland Moodie was once a part. She represents herself as a sacrificial lamb of sorts, whose experiences of loss and alienation might save others from similar hardships: "If these sketches should prove the means of deterring one family from sinking their property, and shipwrecking all their hopes, by going to reside in the backwoods of Canada, I shall consider myself amply repaid for revealing the secrets of the prison-house, and feel that I have not toiled and suffered in the wilderness in vain" (p. 330). The aim of Strickland Moodie's narrative is, like Prince's, pedagogical. But rather than urging her readers to act on behalf of the enslaved, she urges them to save themselves from the kind of emotional and physical suffering she has endured. Beside Strickland Moodie's, Prince's expressions of homesickness seem understated, especially given that Prince's agency was much less and her isolation much greater than Strickland Moodie's. Compared to the Woods' household, the backwoods of Canada was a paradise, not a "prison-house." The understated nature of Prince's longing for home is not because her feelings were less painful than Strickland Moodie's, but because a white, middle-class woman was free to express homesickness in a way that an enslaved Black woman was not.

Compared to Strickland Moodie's, Thomas Pringle's expressions of home-sickness in his South African writings are muted, although home as a domestic space, an affective community, and a native land features importantly in his *African Sketches*. Indeed, one of his aims in emigrating was "to collect again into one social circle, and establish in rural independence, my father's family," or to recreate a familial community that had been driven from its land on the Scottish borders (1834, p. 119). He was deeply aware of what he renounced in emigrating, recollecting "that nearly half the globe's expanse intervened between us and our native land – the homes of our youth, and the friends we had parted from for ever" (p. 126). As Section 4 explores in detail, Pringle's perceptions of the South African landscape and peoples were haunted by memories of Scotland.

Yet the most ardent expressions of homesickness in Pringle's *African Sketches* are displaced onto others, suggesting that he was unwilling to indulge too far in his own person a feminized affective disorder. A striking example of this displacement occurs before the emigrants have landed, as their ship approaches the Cape:

> The sublimely stern aspects of the country … so different from the rich tameness of ordinary English scenery, seemed to strike many of the *Southron* with a degree of awe approaching to consternation. The Scotch, on the contrary, as the stirring recollections of their native land were vividly called up by the rugged peaks and shaggy declivities of this wild coast, were strongly affected, like all true mountaineers on such occasions. Some were excited to extravagant spirits; others silently shed tears. (1834, p. 124)

To the English emigrants aboard ship, the South African terrain is simply foreign, different from the fertile fields they may have known at home. For the Scottish emigrants, by contrast, it is uncanny, at once familiar – reminding them of the Highlands – and strange. Pringle alludes to the theory that inhabitants of mountainous regions are particularly prone to homesickness because their comparative isolation fosters strong attachments (Goodman, 2008, pp. 197–198). The Scottish emigrants thus rejoice at the very resemblances that simultaneously evoke their nostalgic longing for home. At this moment of high emotion, however, Pringle occupies the position of detached observer and does not seem to include himself as one of "the Scotch."

In his poetry, Pringle assumes a variety of voices and perspectives, from those of settlers and slave drivers to those of African Indigenous peoples and the enslaved. Poems such as "The Captive of Camalú" and "The Bechuana Boy," discussed in Section 4, feature Indigenous speakers who mourn for homes destroyed and families brutally murdered by Europeans. As Kenneth McNeil suggests, these poems may reflect Pringle's own feelings of homesickness (2019, pp. 59–63). They also acknowledge that enslaved and dispossessed Indigenous peoples were subject to homesickness too, and that it was therefore not a peculiarly European disease. "The Exile's Lament" is an unequivocal expression of homesickness voiced through a female speaker – a "Scottish Maiden" who "mournfully poured her melting lay / In Teviot's border tongue" (1834, p. 66). Her accented "tongue" marks the speaker's estrangement from the land she perceives as a "howling waste" as she recalls the "uplands green" of the Scottish borders (p. 66). The maiden concludes that

> light, light is poverty's lowliest state,
> On Scotland's peaceful strand,
> Compared with the heart-sick exile's fate
> In this wild and weary land! (p. 67)

Among all of Pringle's poems, this is the only one that represents emigration as an experience of unmitigated fear and loss, so it is significant that those feelings are voiced through a female speaker. By expressing homesickness through the voices of women and Indigenous peoples, Pringle at once portrays it as a weakness to which white men are perhaps less prone and emphasizes Indigenous peoples' capacity for feeling attachment to home. This position, at once condescending and elevating, is characteristic of his writing.

As this section has shown, Strickland Moodie's and Pringle's migrant narratives follow Prince's slave narrative in registering the material and psychological impacts of mobility. In arguing that Prince's *History* was a forerunner of the migrant narrative, then, I do not mean to negate the significant differences between her experiences of forced migration and the experiences of white settlers or sojourners who voluntarily sought to improve the material conditions of their lives. Rather than implying an equivalence among dramatically different experiences of mobility, reading Prince's *History* beside *Roughing It* and *African Sketches* reveals how she used the recounting of her movements to claim a right to homesickness – a right to cultivate attachments to people and places.

3 Representing Slavery in the Colonies and the Metropolis

Upon its publication, *The History of Mary Prince* became embroiled in a struggle to define the truth about slavery in Britain's colonies. In this paper war, which came to a crisis in the early 1830s, accusations of misrepresentation were rife. The sheer distance between Britain and its colonies meant that most Britons could not verify the accuracy of what they read but must trust the eyewitness reports of others. For instance, the *Christian Advocate*, an antislavery periodical that was sympathetic to Prince's plight, observed "the difficulty of proving in this country events which, for the most part, occurred in the West Indies, and proving them, too, by the mouth of a poor uneducated slave" (Thomas, 2005, p. 128). The struggle to control representations of slavery played out across the Anglophone Atlantic world. But, despite London's geographical distance from colonial sites of slavery, works that circulated in the metropolitan literary marketplace held the most weight in defining truths about slavery and bringing about its abolition in Britain's colonies. Thus it was to London that Pringle headed in 1826 to proclaim the injustices that he had witnessed at the Cape. And it was London that James MacQueen visited in 1824, when he worked with the West India Committee – a group of merchants and absentee plantation owners – to refute Thomas Clarkson's *Thoughts on the Necessity of Improving the Conditions of the Slaves in British Colonies* (1823). The first sentences of Pringle's preface to *The History of Mary Prince* indicate Prince's own sense of the possibilities of print publicity that the metropolis offered: "The idea of writing Mary Prince's history was first suggested by herself. She wished it to be done, she said, that good people in England might hear from a slave, what a slave had felt and suffered" (2000, p. 3). Prince's narrative is written from the position of an enslaved colonial subject to free metropolitan readers.

This section explores the relationships between metropolitan and colonial print cultures, specifically in South Africa and the British West Indies, as they were mediated by migrant writers. These writers were uniquely positioned to participate in the debates surrounding abolition because their colonial sojourns endowed them with eyewitness authority in representing slavery to metropolitan readers, while their experiences of colonial print culture impressed upon them the importance of a free press in shaping communal values. Migrant writers not only participated in creating colonial print cultures in their adopted homes, as the story map illustrates, but also constituted a distinct subculture on the margins of the metropolitan literary marketplace.

In what follows, I examine how Pringle's experiences in South Africa prepared him to advocate for abolition not only by exposing him to the horrors of slavery but also by transforming his understanding of the ethical obligations of authorship and highlighting the deficiencies of colonial print culture in contrast to its metropolitan counterpart. Subsequently, I draw on an unlikely source – proslavery writer and former plantation overseer James MacQueen – to conjecture what Mary Prince's exposure to the print cultures of the British West Indies might have been like, and how it might have shaped her desire to publish her narrative in London. Finally, I examine Susanna Strickland's position in the metropolitan literary marketplace both as the ideal consumer of representations of slavery – middle-class, educated, and female – and as a writer whose understanding of authorship was shaped by her conversion to Methodism and the antislavery cause. Although Prince, Pringle, and Strickland looked to "print capitalism as a way of winning English hearts and minds in the struggle to abolish slavery" (Paquet, 2002, p. 38), the specificity of Prince's story was lost and her voice was suppressed as the *History* became a battleground between antislavery and proslavery interests in Britain and its colonies.

3.1 The Colonial Press and the Partisan Politics of Print

When Thomas Pringle undertook the editing and publication of Prince's *History* in 1831, he was no stranger to the power of the printed word to make or break reputations, or to the fact that this power was deeply politicized. He had been involved in the partisan world of publishing since 1817, when William Blackwood invited Pringle and James Cleghorn to edit his new magazine, *Blackwood's*. At this time, Edinburgh rivaled London as a center of literary culture. It was home to the periodicals that shaped Romantic literary tastes, foremost among which were the Whiggish *Edinburgh Review* and the high Tory *Quarterly Review*. Pringle, whose Whig proclivities would lean toward radicalism later in life, was a strange choice for the staunch Tory Blackwood, and it is perhaps not surprising that he and Cleghorn were dismissed from their editorial posts after only six months. After their separation from Blackwood, Pringle and Cleghorn found work rebooting Archibald Constable's flagging *Scots Magazine* as the *Edinburgh Magazine and Literary Miscellany*. This move may have helped Pringle to save face, but he was hurt by the mockery of John Wilson and John Gibson Lockhart, whom Blackwood had recruited to relaunch his magazine, and who depicted him in the infamous Chaldee Manuscript as a crippled lamb (Vigne, 2012, p. 36). It was entirely in keeping with this satire of Edinburgh's literary figures to highlight Pringle's bodily infirmity, singling out the lameness caused by a childhood accident as a symbol of editorial ineptitude. Philip Flynn's claim that Pringle and Cleghorn's issues of *Blackwood's* were "flat," with "no fizz, no flash," seems harsh, but for a new magazine to compete in Edinburgh's crowded periodical market "strategic and occasional excess" was necessary (2006, pp. 142, 137). Wilson and Lockhart, whose social standing was more secure than Pringle's or Cleghorn's, were willing to take risks that might bring "attention, interest, even notoriety" to the magazine (p. 138).

Although bruised by his treatment in *Blackwood's*, Pringle was unwilling to renounce his authorial ambitions when he emigrated. But the settlement of Glen Lynden in the upper Baviaans River valley was hundreds of miles from Cape Town, and its isolation prevented Pringle from contributing to his family's income "by writing books and literary articles sent to London," as he had hoped to do (1966, p. xxxvii). Yet "The Emigrant's Cabin" suggests that Pringle's time in Glen Lynden was not devoid of literary culture and was essential to the development of his antislavery sentiments and to the rejuvenation of his love of literature. Written around 1822 but not published until 1834, the poem is addressed to Pringle's friend John Fairbarn. In it, Pringle imagines how Fairbarn, who was at the time considering emigration, might respond if he were suddenly transported to Glen Lynden. Fairbarn is impressed with the material comforts that Pringle and his wife enjoy but nonetheless affirms his preference for a "poetic den" located "within reach of Books and Men" (1834, p. 40). Implying that material comforts are surely less important than intellectual sustenance, Fairbarn asserts that "The MIND requires fit exercise and food / Not to be found 'mid Afric's deserts rude" (p. 40), and asks Pringle disbelievingly,

> Was it for Nature's wants, fire, shelter, food,
> You sought this dreary, soulless solitude?
> Broke off your ties with men of cultured mind,
> Your native land, your early friends resigned? (p. 41)

Fairbarn cannot imagine living at such a distance from centers of European culture and assumes that Pringle must feel the want of intellectual exchange. Yet Pringle assures him that "even in my desert-den, / I still hold intercourse with thinking men." Among various sources of intellectual camaraderie he mentions Landdrost Strockenstrom of Graaff Reinet, who "though in this wild country born and bred, / Is able in affairs, in books well read," and "the gay-humored Captain Fox":

> With whom I roamed 'mid Koonap's woods and rocks
> From Winterberg to Gola's savage grot
> Talking of Rogers, Campbell, Coleridge, Scott. (pp. 43–44)

While Pringle enjoys the company of these men who share his literary tastes, he also implies that his priorities have changed somewhat since his emigration.

More "meritorious" than Strockenstrom's knowledge of literature is that he is a "zealous friend to Afric's swarthy race" (1834, p. 43). Pringle quickly learned that settler society had no place for the solitary cultivation of genius or the dazzling displays of wit that might have charmed Edinburgh's literati. Instead, he intends to use his talents as a writer "for the sad Natives of the soil, / By stern oppression doomed to scorn and toil" (p. 45). Rather than an end in itself, authorship became for Pringle a means to effect the emancipation of the Indigenous peoples of the Cape who had been turned from their land and bound into servitude by European settlers.

It is unsurprising, then, that when Pringle was appointed the librarian at the South African Public Library in Cape Town, he was determined to use his position there to promote the acquisition of practical knowledge among settlers and advocate for the abolition of slavery in South Africa. The library had been founded by a bequest from a Dutch settler, Joachim von Dessin; according to Colonel William Bird, a colonial official, it included "the best ancient and most recent modern publications in religion, in the classics, in history, poetry, geography, chemistry, and political economy; a most ample collection of essays, voyages, and travels; and dictionaries of all ages and languages" (Bird, 1823, p. 145). Despite its impressive holdings, the library revealed to Colonel Bird a dearth of cultural refinement at Cape Town. He observed, "the thing that appears to be chiefly wanting, which Mr Dessin could not bequeath, is a collection of readers; for reading is not an African passion" (p. 146). When John Fairbarn, the addressee of "The Emigrant's Cabin," joined Pringle in Cape Town, the two men determined to create a colonial readership by opening an academy for settlers' sons and founding a literary and philosophical society for Cape Town's mercantile and professional classes. Furthermore, by starting a monthly magazine and a weekly newspaper, they would not simply shape the tastes and views of this formative readership but also transform Cape Town "into a version of an intellectual, educational, scientific and publishing centre on the Edinburgh model" (MacKenzie, 2012, p. 70). In short, Pringle and Fairbarn hoped to develop at Cape Town an autonomous provincial print culture – one that, while inevitably limited in scope, would function independently of the London literary marketplace.

Pringle and Fairbarn did not need Benedict Anderson's *Imagined Communities* (1983) to convince them that the press was crucial in developing a settler colonial identity, a culture that mimicked but never successfully replicated that of the diasporic homeland. Britons who emigrated to South Africa generally did not consider themselves temporary sojourners who would eventually return home, but instead as permanent settlers who would build new lives for themselves and their descendants. In the prospectus for their *South African Journal*, Pringle and Fairbarn promised that the periodical would promote the "consolidation of native feelings, sentiments, and views into a distinct and pervading character," so that settlers would no longer feel themselves "a disunited, wavering, and temporary assemblage of adventurers, with our ultimate views rooted beyond the ATLANTIC" (1824, n.p.). It would create this cultural coherence by serving on one hand as a source of local information, with essays on "subjects connected immediately with this Colony, such as its Commerce, Statistics, &c," and on the other hand as an arbitrator of cultural value, offering readers "miscellaneous Papers, on Literary and Philosophical

Subjects" (n.p.). The first issue of the journal embodies this bifurcated focus: an essay "On the Writings of Wordsworth" and two unsigned poems by Pringle jostle against a report on the colonies of New South Wales and Van Diemen's Land, and an article "On Literary and Scientific Societies," outlining the benefits such societies might offer Cape Town, precedes a "how-to" article on the "Cultivation of Tobacco," which proposes the plant as a lucrative crop for the Cape.

Whether the *South African Journal* would have succeeded in creating a sense of "self-respect, and home-importance" among European colonists at the Cape remains unknown, as it ceased publication after only two issues. Pringle's reason for so abruptly aborting the *South African Journal* was Governor Charles Somerset's attempt to regulate what was printed in the colony. Aware of the volatility of certain topics at the Cape, Pringle and Fairbarn had determined to avoid personal attacks, party politics, and "topics likely to excite violent controversy in the colony, such as the Slavery question, the condition of the Aborigines, &c." (Pringle, 1834, pp. 319–320). While they eschewed *Blackwood's* polemics as a strategy for exciting readers' interest, they also agreed "never to compromise our birth-right as British subjects by editing any publication under a censorship" (p. 322). When it came to rights and liberties, including freedom of expression, Pringle was quick to claim Britishness even though he was editing a colonial publication.

The first issue of the *South African Journal* hints at the tensions developing between Somerset and Pringle. An unsigned poem by Pringle on "the Proscription of a Free Press in Germany and Switzerland" is clearly pointed at Somerset, demanding that "under Britain's guardian shield, / Law, Freedom, Truth, begin their reign" (1824b, p. 9). The essay "On Literary and Scientific Societies," probably written by Fairbarn, informs readers that these organizations are second only to "the Liberty of the Press" in ensuring the "personal, civil, and religious liberty, enjoyed by the mass of the people in all the Christian States" (p. 54). Randolph Vigne explains that Somerset demonstrated extreme "watchfulness against any sign of radicalism at the Cape and a deadly dread of the press as a fomenter of revolt" (2012, p. 121). Pringle and Fairbarn's plan to establish a society that would promote the exchange of knowledge must have worried Somerset, who implemented what Pringle described as "the Cape 'Reign of Terror'" – a "frightful system of espionage" intended "to strike down every man who should dare even to *look* or *think* disapprobation" of the colonial government (1834, p. 323). As one of the emigrants sponsored by a home government anxious to rid Britain of radicals in the wake of Peterloo, Pringle was a prime target for the governor's suspicions, which were first awakened when Pringle was appointed secretary for the Society for the Relief of Distressed Settlers in 1823. Erratic storms and floods had damaged crops and left recent British settlers in the district of Albany in a state of extreme "poverty and privation" (Pringle, 1824a, p. 29). Pringle produced *Some Account of the Present State of the English Settlers of Albany, South Africa* (1824), a compilation of testimonials framed by his own account of the conditions in Albany, to raise money for the eponymous settlers. Published in London, the pamphlet raised an impressive £10,000 in support of the struggling settlers. But its criticisms of the colonial administration's response to four consecutive years of crop failure, although worded diplomatically, must have offended Somerset, who, as Pringle explained in a letter to Walter Scott, decided that Pringle was "a violent Whig" and "an arrant dissenter" – possibly the worst slurs that the high Tory governor could come up with (Vigne, 2011, p. 76).

Pringle's literary ambitions threatened to overturn a precedent that had lasted "since the earliest days of British rule at the Cape" when the colonial government had assumed oversight of the only press (MacKenzie, 2012, p. 70). In 1822, when Pringle took up his position as librarian, Cape Town's only newspaper, the *Cape Town Gazette*, was published by the government. Pringle had learned in Edinburgh that periodicals were political as much as literary publications. Yet the difference in power between William Blackwood and Pringle was nothing compared to the disparity between Somerset and Pringle. In addition to the challenges common to other settler colonial print cultures – a lack of infrastructure and equipment and a dearth of people with the money to purchase printed materials and the time to read them – writers and publishers at the Cape faced the additional hurdle of government regulation. Finding himself denounced by Somerset "as a turbulent and factious person, and a marked disturber of the Government" (Vigne, 2011, p. 207), Pringle left his post at the library, shut down the *South African Journal*, and determined to redirect his rhetorical energies toward the imperial center. Before he could return to Britain, however, he would need to settle his significant debts and come up with the money for his passage.

During the interval between leaving Cape Town in 1824 and sailing for London in early 1826, Pringle wrote much of the poetry that he would publish and republish in periodicals and gift annuals in England and South Africa over the ensuing decade. Yet Pringle no longer sought to win fame as a poet, as he might have done when he published his first collection of poems, *Autumnal Excursions* (1819). Instead, he approached authorship pragmatically, regarding writing as a way both of making a living and of furthering the antislavery cause. Pringle explained to Fairbairn that although he still hoped "to write something that may not dishonour Scotland," he felt almost "criminal in giving up any part of my heart or time to poetry" while ethnic conflicts at the Cape continued unresolved (Vigne, 2011, pp. 192, 198). Accordingly, as Section 4 shows, much of the poetry that Pringle wrote at this time sought to give voice to the Indigenous African peoples who had been dispossessed of their land and enslaved by European settlers. Once settled in London, however, Pringle renounced poetry for editorial work, which offered the pleasing prospect of a regular income and the opportunity to promote an antislavery agenda.

The printing press was crucial to British imperial expansion, but the norms and practices of metropolitan print culture were not simply exported wholesale to the colonies; rather, as Tony Ballantyne explains, they were "contested and reworked in each colonial context" (2007, p. 343). A comparison of this "reworking" in South Africa and the British West Indies, both of which employed slave labor, reveals some basic similarities. Countering the long-standing assumption that the British West Indies were unaffected by Enlightenment-era cosmopolitanism, James Robertson (2014) has argued that ephemeral forms of print – newspapers, gazettes, instructional manuals, and the pamphlets in which the institution of slavery was debated – facilitated the exchange of ideas both within the region and between the colony and the metropolis. However, the degree to which slaves were impacted by or participated in this exchange is an open question. Leah Thomas (2019) has drawn attention to Prince's "knowledge networks," the communal means through which Prince may have acquired information she imparts in the *History*, including her trading connections, her church, and her encounters with the law. These networks of oral communication among enslaved and free Blacks ran parallel to and sometimes intersected with the print networks that Robertson describes. Indeed, print may well have been one of the sources of Prince's knowledge for some of the details that Thomas attributes to oral transmission; Prince was taught some basic reading skills by both her young charge, Miss Fanny Pruden, and the "Moravian ladies" in Antigua (2000, pp. 9, 29). While we cannot recover Prince's exposure to print with any more certainty than we can identify the individuals in her "knowledge networks," it is none-theless worth exploring how the print cultures of the British West Indies might have shaped her belief that print could be a powerful tool in persuading "good people in England . . . what a slave had felt and suffered" (p. 3).

Roderick Cave reminds us that the West Indies "is not a unit; each island had its distinctive political and cultural history, just as it had its own racial and religious mix" (1978, p. 164). As the story map illustrates, the availability of printed material also differed substantially from one island to another. For instance, printing was not introduced to Turks Islands, where Prince worked in the salt ponds during her enslavement by Mr. D–, until the 1840s (p. 164). By contrast, Benjamin Franklin facilitated the establishment of a press in

Antigua, where Prince was enslaved by Mr. and Mrs. Wood for thirteen years, almost a century earlier, in 1748 (p. 168). By the end of the eighteenth century, all the large islands had at least one printer and issued weekly newspapers, the contents of which would have included advertisements of slave auctions and notices about runaway slaves, along with news from Britain and Europe. In the British West Indies as in South Africa, print publication was controlled by the white population, with the first newspapers for free Blacks emerging only in the early 1830s, on the eve of the abolition of slavery (p. 171). And much like the press at the Cape, printing in the West Indies often was introduced under the auspices of the colonial government (p. 168), which exacerbated perceptions of bias and censorship. Bradford Swan explains that a "little pressure" from colonial administrators "was all that was needed to bring any rebellious newspaper or printer into line" (1970, p. 43). While Swan's research shows that colonial officials generally sided with the planter aristocracy, James MacQueen declared that these officials – and the British metropolitan government they represented – were under the thumb of antislavery advocates.

Indeed, if MacQueen's account of colonial West Indian print culture is to be trusted, Prince would have had reason to regard print as a potent weapon in the fight for emancipation. In an article for the proslavery *Blackwood's Magazine*, MacQueen claimed that colonial officials in the British West Indies routinely censored publications that were critical of abolition. In Mauritius, he declared, "the press is completely under the control of the Governor, whose Secretary is its Master and the Censor," and who prohibits the publication of articles that "might reflect disgrace upon our African brethren" (1831a, p. 206). Similarly, he avers that the *Guiana Chronicle* had been permitted to continue publication in Demerara only on the condition of "Abstinence from all comments on the slave question, *except* such as are calculated to *promote the measures recommended by his Majesty's government* and sanctioned by Parliament!" (1831c, p. 756). MacQueen felt that the colonial press, although locally controlled, reflected the interests and values of a distant and uniformed metropolitan England rather than those of colonists. For instance, the *Guiana Chronicle* "was to support every act emanating from government which had emancipation in view, without any reference to the property of the master, the comfort of the slaves, or the actual safety of the colony!" (p. 756). MacQueen informs readers that "the official gazettes of the Crown Colonies are all thus chained, and must ... dance in fetters to any tune which Aldermanbury may drive Downing Street to play" (p. 756). The image of chained and fettered newspapers suggests that the colonial press is enslaved, held captive, ironically, by the antislavery interest. It is an image that might have surprised Pringle and Prince.

Issuing his critique of the colonial press in the pages of *Blackwood's*, MacQueen reached a readership that was likely to have been receptive to his complaints. As MacQueen observed in a letter to William Blackwood, the magazine's proslavery stance had helped *Blackwood's* achieve a "great circulation" in the Caribbean (Thomas, 2005, p. 117). The very terminology that MacQueen employs in *Blackwood's* emphasizes the fundamental differences between those who sought and those who opposed the abolition of slavery. MacQueen refers to members of the London Anti-Slavery Society as "anti-colonial calumniators" or simply "anti-colonials," conflating their opposition to slavery with an opposition to British imperial expansion (1831a, p. 186). In MacQueen's rendition, moreover, the slave system is "not a political party question, but a question relating exclusively to property – to the property of men of all parties" (p. 186). By reducing slaves to "property," MacQueen not only dehumanizes them but also suggests that the abolition of slavery would render other forms of personal property vulnerable. David Lambert explains that "MacQueen's significance within the slavery controversy lay not so much in the particular proslavery discourses that he articulated through his writing, but in his central place" in a proslavery network developed "through correspondence and publication, [and] through the traffic in commodities and wealth" (2008, p. 406). MacQueen was in many senses Pringle's proslavery counterpart, a well-connected editor and writer who brought eyewitness accounts of colonial slavery to metropolitan readers.

3.2 Gender and Race in the Metropolitan Literary Marketplace

The History of Mary Prince constituted a node at which MacQueen's proslavery network intersected with Pringle's antislavery network, and colonial print cultures met in the literary metropolis. Pringle's and MacQueen's colonial sojourns revealed to them the political agendas that shaped representations of slavery, but these were not always apparent to metropolitan readers. When Susanna Strickland first met Pringle, she was just such a metropolitan reader. Her account of her awakening in the preface to Ashton Warner's *Negro Slavery Described by a Negro* suggests the importance of one form of evidence that the proslavery interests could not easily muster in support of their position – first-person testimony from enslaved people. Strickland recorded Ashton Warner's narrative shortly before Mary Prince's. *Negro Slavery Described by a Negro* has received less attention than *The History of Mary Prince*, perhaps because Warner died before his account saw print. Its appearance in the world was attended with none of the refutations and legal cases that Prince's *History* evoked. The publication of *Negro Slavery* sheds light both on Strickland's conversion from a proslavery to an antislavery position and on Pringle's editorial interventions in Prince's narrative, which are absent from Warner's. It illuminates what the antislavery cause sought to achieve by putting enslaved people's stories in print and how they understood the possibilities and pitfalls of publication in the metropolitan literary marketplace.

Strickland's conversion to the antislavery cause is worth exploring in some detail, as she belonged to both MacQueen's and Prince's target audience of middle-class women. Indeed, she was in some ways their ideal reader. On one hand, proslavery writers appealed to those who shared her family's social pretensions and Tory leanings by declaring the sanctity of hierarchy and property. On the other hand, antislavery writers appealed to her feminine sensibilities and newly awakened religious zeal by offering carefully sanitized depictions of the sufferings of enslaved peoples.

When, in 1829, Pringle first made Strickland's acquaintance, she was in the midst of what John Thurston has described as a "moral and religious crisis" that called into question her vocation as a writer (Thurston, 1996, p. 30). Strickland had hitherto followed the lead of her elder sisters Elizabeth and Agnes, who wrote for periodicals with a Church and Crown bias including *La Belle Assemblée*, the *Lady's Magazine*, and the *Court Magazine*, and whose allegiance to their father's high church, Tory sensibilities was later displayed in their multivolume *Lives of the Queens of England* (1840–1848). It is unsurprising, given this background, that Susanna Strickland derived her earliest opinions on slavery "chiefly from literary periodicals on the side of the planters, such as the *Quarterly Review*, *Blackwood's Magazine*, and other publications of the same class; works certainly but little calculated to excite the feelings or alarm the conscience on this momentous question" (Warner, 1831, p. 6). *Blackwood's* and the *Quarterly* catered to an educated, relatively wealthy, and predominantly male readership, and they were committed to supporting a political establishment and social hierarchy that their readers perceived as under threat from abolitionists and those who supported the extension of the franchise. However, Strickland acknowledged that these journals were far from the only ones to support the perpetuation of slavery, observing that the West Indian interest's "corrupt influence over a large majority of the lighter vehicles of popular information has enabled them to gain possession of the public ear, and to abuse public credulity, to an extent not generally appreciated" (pp. 5–6). These "lighter vehicles" included some of the magazines to which Strickland's elder sisters introduced her, and to which she became a contributor.

When Susanna Strickland converted from Anglicanism to Methodism, alienating her elder sisters in the process, she began to question her aims as an author and regretted having "employed those abilities with which heaven had endowed me, doubtless for a wise and useful purpose, entirely for my own amusement, without any wish to benefit and improve my fellow creatures" (Ballstadt et al., 1985, p. 50). The man she would come to call Papa Pringle – although he was only fourteen years her elder – offered her just such a purpose in the evangelical antislavery movement. It may have been as a writer for *Friendship's Offering*, a literary annual that Pringle edited from 1829 until his death in 1834, that Strickland began to see authorship as a way to support the antislavery movement. The primary audience for literary annuals was middle-class evangelically inclined women, which was also, according to Clare Midgley, one of the most active constituents of the antislavery movement (1992, pp. 92–115). While these annuals were often prized more for their lavish illustrations than their literary content, Pringle exploited the genre's appeal for middle-class women by including pieces that might further the antislavery cause. For instance, the 1830 volume of *Friendship's Offering* includes Pringle's own "The Bechuana Boy," James Montgomery's "The Cry from South Africa," and an unsigned poem titled "The African." Strickland began to contribute to *Friendship's Offering* in 1830, having already published a few poems in *The Athenaeum* while it was briefly under Pringle's editorship. Around this time, she also exchanged *La Belle Assemblée* for more morally earnest evangelical publications such as the *Ecclesiastic* and the *Amulet*.

It was while she was "domesticated with [her] dear adopted father, Mr. Pringle" that Strickland took down the narratives of Mary Prince and Ashton Warner. In January 1831, she wrote to a friend,

> I have been writing Mr. Pringle's black Mary's life from her own dictation and for her benefit adhering to her own simple story and language without . . . flourish or romance. It is a pathetic little history and is now printing in the form of a pamphlet to be laid before the Houses of Parliament. Of course my name does not appear. Mr. Pringle has added a very interesting appendix and I hope the work will do much good. (Ballstadt et al., 1985, p. 57)

It may have been humbling for a writer self-confessedly struggling to subdue her own "vanity and presumption" to serve as the anonymous secretary to as inglorious a Milton as Mary Prince, limited to taking down Prince's words with adding flourishes of her own (p. 50). Ryan Hanley has suggested that Strickland saw her role as Prince's amanuensis as an opportunity to "break into the London literary scene" (2019, p. 80). It is true that Prince's *History* sold better than anything Strickland had written. But in suggesting that Strickland was motivated by the possibility of fame, Hanley attributes to her a cynicism that she almost certainly did not feel. Indeed, her compliance with practices that systematically marginalized women writers in the metropolitan literary market-place suggests that Strickland might have feared the attention that her recording of Prince's narrative might bring. Strickland's career began with the anonymous publication of *Spartacus, a Roman Story* in 1822, and until the publication of *Enthusiasm, and Other Poems* (1831), most of her work appeared anonymously, under the initials S.S. or Z.Z., or under a pseudonym. This was by no means unusual for women writers at a time when publication sat uneasily with ideals of middle-class feminine propriety. Recording Prince's narrative may have cemented Strickland's place in the evangelical antislavery community to which Pringle had introduced her, but it is unlikely that she saw it as a step on the ladder to literary fame.

Between her religious conversion in 1829 and her emigration to Canada in 1832, Strickland began to develop an authorial identity quite different from her elder sisters' – one that was evangelical both in doctrine and in style. Central to her new conception of authorship was the belief in the potential of print to promote social reform, including the abolition of slavery. In the preface to Warner's *Negro Slavery Described by a Negro*, Strickland offers an account of her own conversion to the antislavery cause as a model for readers and a corrective to the "misinformation" spread "by those interested in maintaining the West India system" (Warner, 1831, p. 5). She explains that her beliefs about slavery were transformed by "the frequent opportunities which Providence recently and unexpectedly threw in my way, of conversing with several negroes, both male and female, who had been British colonial slaves, and who had borne in their own persons the marks of the brand and the whip . . . To their simple and unaffecting narratives I could not listen unmoved" (p. 11). Strickland partici-pates in what Dwight McBride describes as the fetishization of the enslaved person's unspeakable knowledge of slavery by positioning herself as a kind of second-order witness (2001, pp. 89–94). Although she could not personally testify to the horrors of slavery, she could testify to the impact of hearing formerly enslaved peoples describe them and of seeing the marks left on their bodies. Convinced by her own eyes and ears of the atrocities of slavery, Strickland "resolved no longer to be an accomplice in its criminality, though it were only by keeping silence regarding it" (Warner, 1831, p. 11). She was inspired to record Warner's story, "thinking that the same means which had operated so effectually on my own mind might produce a favorable result in other persons" (p. 11). Strickland's efforts to yoke the power of print to the abolitionist movement was not limited to the recording of slave narratives. *Enthusiasm*, a collection of poems published a few months after Prince's *History*, includes "Appeal to the Free," a poem written on behalf of a "heart-broken slave" (Strickland, 1831, p. 79). The poem perhaps owes its being to

Strickland's interactions with Prince and Warner. Channeling the evangelical zeal that brought Strickland to the antislavery movement, it reminds readers that "Christians, enlightened with precepts divine" will not "suffer a brother in bondage to pine" (p. 79).

Strickland played a part in the debates surrounding the representation of slavery first as a metropolitan reader trying to make sense of competing accounts, and only subsequently as a writer and witness to the testimony of the formerly enslaved. While she has received some attention for her part in the publication of Prince's *History* (e.g., Gadpaille, 2016; Whitlock, 2000), the role she plays in Warner's *Negro Slavery Described by a Negro* has been overlooked. Unlike Prince, Warner was not a resident of Pringle's household, and Strickland took down his story in a Greenwich hospital. *Negro Slavery Described by a Negro* is unusual in that it is presented to readers entirely under the auspices of a white woman. Strickland assumes sole responsibility for editing the narrative, explaining, "I have adhered strictly to the simple facts, adopting, wherever it could conveniently be done, his own language, which for a person in his condition, is remarkably expressive and appropriate" (Warner, 1831, p. 15). Ashton Warner's narrative is subject to much less textual buttressing than Mary Prince's. The text does include a deed of manumission, but there are no letters attesting to Warner's character, no letters from the executors of his enslaver, the recently deceased Mr. Wilson, and no interventions by Thomas Pringle. However, *Negro Slavery Described by a Negro* does include "an Appendix Containing the Testimony of four Christian Ministers," all of whom had spent time in the British West Indies. Whereas the appendices in Prince's narrative immediately concern her character and the truth of her claims, these clerical testimonies do not relate to Ashton Warner's account in particular but are rather descriptions of West Indian slavery in general. The relative autonomy granted to Warner's narrative may reflect the unavailability of supporting documents, but gender undoubtedly also made a difference to the presentation of his story. While Prince's assertions of sexual autonomy, a form of personal agency, were scrupulously excluded from the *History*, Strickland's preface draws readers' attention to Warner's agency. When he runs away or stands up to his master, Warner asserts "his independence with the resolution and spirit which a sense of justice and a love of liberty alone can give" (p. 13). Prince, by contrast, must show Christian fortitude under suffering to prove herself worthy of liberty. Much as Warner is commended for standing up for his right to freedom, so his story is allowed to stand with comparatively little commentary.

Strickland's preface to *Negro Slavery Described by a Negro* testifies to the potential impact of first-person accounts of slavery, indicating what she and Pringle may have hoped to achieve by giving voice to Warner and Prince. The preface also illustrates the part that the antislavery cause played in Strickland's reconceptualization of herself as an author, as she sought to become less like her elder sisters and more like Pringle. Her single-handed presentation of Warner's narrative to the public also illuminates the hierarchy of authority structuring the metropolitan literary marketplace. As a white woman, Strickland could underwrite the testimony of a Black man seemingly without any implications of impropriety – although it is difficult to imagine that her elder sisters were entirely happy with her accomplishment. But the testimony of a Black *woman* was more problematic, and Strickland was relegated to a less prominent role in the publication of Prince's *History* – that of silent amanuensis.

The furor caused by the publication of *The History of Mary Prince* illustrates the power of print to affect and engage readers from Scotland to the West Indies. At a time when "black writers faced a book trade that privileged whiteness and granted them access most often through patrons, editors, and amanuenses" (Rezek, 2015, p. 21), Pringle and Strickland gave Prince a voice – albeit a mediated one – in the metropolitan literary marketplace. Published just as Parliament was about to begin debating unconditional abolition, Prince's *History* became one of the antislavery movement's strongest weapons in the battle to represent the truth of slavery. The *Anti-Slavery Monthly Reporter*, a periodical edited by Pringle and Zachary Macaulay, regularly included first-person accounts of slavery, including some by female slaves, but these were briefer than Prince's. As a stand-alone pamphlet, *The History of Mary Prince* was more prominent than the narratives published in the *Anti-Slavery Reporter* and more vulnerable to attack. Hanley argues that the libel trials following the publication of the *History* were "an extension of the *History* itself" (2019, p. 96), and the same might be said of the responses to Prince's narrative published in *Blackwood's*, the *Glasgow Courier*, and the *Bermuda Royal Gazette*. Both the trials and the written commentary were "ultimately less concerned with the factual bases of Prince's narrative than how her character was represented" (p. 96). Prince's character in turn became implicated in the debate over the accuracy of representations of slavery circulating in the metropolis. Prince herself was written out of the war of words instigated by the publication of *History*.

The concerted attempts of John Wood and James MacQueen to discredit the *History* as, in the latter's words, "a venomous Anti-colonial Manifesto" suggest that Pringle's sense of the vulnerability of Prince's narrative was not misplaced, although his efforts to bolster its authority may have been. For MacQueen, the *History* was just one more example of "the total disregard for truth which rules the enemies of the Colonies in every publication which they put forth" (1831b, p. 454). He ascribes to Prince's narrative the dual purposes of "destroying the character of two respectable individuals, her owners, MR AND MRS WOOD of Antigua" and "undermin[ing] our colonial empire" (1831c, 744). In fact, MacQueen was less concerned with clearing the reputation of Prince's enslavers than with defending the slave system on which their wealth and power had been built. In an article published in the *Glasgow Courier* on April 21, 1832, MacQueen made this point explicitly, declaring that "the life and character of those two respectable individuals are most cruelly calumniated, vilified, mis-represented, and libelled by the basest falsehoods and most obvious untruths; and through them, as was the chief object [of *The History of Mary Prince*], the character of the whole white population in the Colonies is sought to be black-ened and assailed" (p. 1). Three thousand miles away, the *Bermuda Royal Gazette* echoed MacQueen's defense of the Woods, and by implication, of all West Indian enslavers. An article titled "The Anti-Slavery Society and the West India Colonists" self-righteously declared that "One of the most important duties of the public press is the refutation of calumnies, and the protection of injured individuals and communities from slanderous and infamous attacks" (1831, p. 1) Accordingly it sought to defend "Mr. Wood and the West India colonists," whom Prince's *History* "held up to the scorn of the whole world, as fiends guilty of every diabolical atrocity" (p. 1). While the article has nothing kind to say about Prince, the primary target of its vitriol is Pringle as secretary of the Anti-Slavery Society. As the article's title suggests, the *Royal Gazette* places the publication of the *History* at the center of a struggle between the London-based Anti-Slavery Society and the planters of the West Indies for the authority to represent slavery.

As Prince was rendered silent and invisible in this struggle, the proslavery interests' objections to the *History* grew louder and more visible. Until late in the nineteenth century, it was the common practice for articles in *Blackwood's* to appear anonymously or pseudonymously, but most unusually MacQueen's proslavery articles were published under his own name. Perhaps, as MacQueen's proslavery sentiments became increasingly unpopular and his claims increasingly outrageous, William Blackwood was content to distance his magazine from them slightly. In one of the innuendoes that punctuate his *Blackwood's* article on the *History*, MacQueen promises readers that he will "extract ... Pringle's sting and Pringle's venom, out of Mary's tale" (1831c, p. 744). This pun on "tail" implies that Prince and Pringle carried on an illicit sexual relationship while she was employed as a servant in his household, where, according to MacQueen, "she was frequently called to his closet to give a narrative of the severities inflicted upon her by several owners, but more especially by her last owners, Mr and Mrs Wood" (p. 745). Remarks like these would have made MacQueen an easy target for a lawsuit had his residence in

Glasgow, outside the jurisdiction of the Court of Common Pleas, not placed him out of Pringle's reach. MacQueen's accusation that the *History* had ruined the reputation of Prince's owner John Wood led Pringle to bring a libel suit instead against Thomas Cadell, *Blackwood's* London publisher. Although Pringle was awarded only £5 in damages and coverage of his legal fees rather than the £2,000 he had requested, his victory was not merely symbolic. Cadell recognized that Pringle's legal actions represented more than an attempt to protect his own reputation and that the real target of the writ was neither himself nor MacQueen, but rather West Indian enslavers (Lambert, 2008, p. 400). The failure of MacQueen's West Indian supporters to cover his costs in the case, as he had believed they would, indicates the decline of his influence. Moreover, following the lawsuit, Cadell's lawyer assumed the responsibility of vetting all MacQueen's contributions to *Blackwood's* for potential libels before they were published, an arrangement that effectively eliminated his voice from the magazine for almost a decade (p. 402). But when MacQueen instigated a retaliatory lawsuit, with James Wood suing Pringle for libel, Prince was called to take the stand as a witness and her sexual history was made public.

David Lambert argues that Prince's *History* played an important role "in disturbing MacQueen's networked proslavery advocacy" (2008, p. 407). But this achievement came at the cost of the erasure of the specificity of Prince's story, which was lost in the struggle between antislavery and proslavery writers to represent the truth of slavery. Moreover, the publication of the *History* did not realize Prince's hope of returning to Antigua a free woman. But Prince did manage to communicate what was, to her, the truth of slavery:

> I will say the truth to English people who may read this history that my good friend, Miss S–, is now writing down for me. The man that says slaves be quite happy in slavery – that they don't want to be free – that man is either ignorant or a lying person. I never heard a slave say so, till I heard tell of it in England. (2000, p. 38)

Prince affirmed this point through her decision to remain in England despite the prospect of continued poverty, loneliness, and public disparagement. This is the only point at which Prince alludes to Strickland in the *History*, reminding readers of the antislavery network that brought her story to public attention. What happened to these "good friend[s]" once Prince's sexual history was brought to light? Did they stand by her or abandon her as no longer useful to their aims? Did she return to Antigua after enslaved peoples were emancipated on August 1, 1834? Or did she die in obscurity? Prince's name appears only briefly in the extant letters of Pringle and Strickland following the publication of her *History*, and no mention is made of her fate. The biases of historical archives, and perhaps too of Prince's antislavery friends, are evident in her absence; despite the paper wars generated by her *History*, Mary Prince appears no more in print.

4 Migration, Dispossession, and Slavery

How did Thomas Pringle's and Susanna Strickland Moodie's collaboration on Mary Prince's *History* influence their thinking about race and migration more generally? Did it represent a departure for Pringle from his previous writings about slavery? And did it leave any discernible mark on Strickland Moodie's later work? There is no doubt that Pringle and Strickland Moodie were committed to the antislavery cause, but they held with this commitment a belief that it was Britain's duty to civilize the savage and convert the heathen. Moreover, as settlers in Britain's colonies, Pringle and Strickland Moodie participated in the displacement of Black and Indigenous peoples from their hereditary lands. They did not see the inconsistencies between their positions as abolitionists and settler colonialists that are so apparent from a historical distance. For, as Douglas Lorimer observes, "The abolitionists' concern for the slave did not necessarily lead to the acceptance of the free Negro as a brother and equal" (1978, p. 35). This section explores the continuities and tensions between Pringle's and Strickland Moodie's collaboration on Prince's *History* and their representations of race and migration elsewhere in their work as they negotiated their positions as at once dispossessed and dispossessors. While Pringle deplored the impact of colonial settlement on South African Indigenous peoples, he saw a viable alternative in the domestic Christian colonialism that he modeled through his incorporation of the former slaves Marossi and Mary Prince into his household. Strickland Moodie's fiction suggests that she too was aware of the connections between British colonial migration and settlement and the exploitation of Indigenous peoples, but the challenges of her own experiences as a settler ultimately supplanted her concerns with the impact of British migration on others.

4.1 Clearances and Colonial Domesticity

Thomas Pringle's experiences illustrate the causal connection between Scottish dispossession and emigration and the forced removal of Indigenous peoples from their land. He explored this connection in his poetry and prose by invoking two versions of Scottishness, one defined by the domesticity and patriarchal piety enshrined in Robert Burns's "The Cotter's Saturday Night," and the other defined by Walter Scott's noble but savage Highlanders – one, in other words, associated with dwelling and the other with depopulation. Governor Charles

Somerset had strategically placed the Scottish settlers at Glen Lynden to protect the so-called Neutral Ground from which the Khoi and the Xhosa had been driven in the Frontier War of 1818–1819. Lord Somerset's administration decided that Scots, with their history of cattle reiving and border wars, would be particularly well suited to develop this region while also defending the colony's outskirts (Vigne, 2012, p. 48). Pringle referred to the frequent conflicts in the region as "our Cape border-wars" and jokingly described himself as a "petty 'border chief'" who could "muster upwards of thirty armed horsemen ... at an hour's notice" (1834, pp. 217, 238). Sometimes Pringle's "troops" intervened in tribal conflicts to protect the Khoi or Xhosa from the attacks of the San Bushmen, and at other times they defended themselves from similar depredations. Over time, Pringle came to regard the Bushmen as victims rather than aggressors, recognizing that their "savage and predatory habits" were a result of dispossession and an alternative to a life spent in "servitude to the Boors" (Vigne, 2011, p. 244). Nonetheless, Glen Lynden, along with the other settlements of 1820, was "instrumental in the dispossession of African peoples: it served to produce endemic and brutal violence where it was supposed to bring peace" (MacKenzie, 2012, p. 48).

This "brutal violence" is entirely absent from "The Emigrant's Song," a bucolic celebration of South African bounty. Sarah Sharp (2019) has revealed the indebtedness of poetic representations of Scottish settler domesticity to Robert Burns's "The Cotter's Saturday Night," observing that these representations flourished at precisely the moment when the introduction of modern agricultural methods were driving the semi-independent cotter class from Scotland. "The Emigrant's Song" shares this indebtedness, celebrating the simple domestic virtues that Scottish settlers bring to their new homes across the globe. The poet asks his beloved "Maid of the Tweed" to accompany him to "the wilds of South-Africa," where he will build them a "home, like a beehive," a reference both to the round, dome-like shape of settlers' huts and to the industriousness of their inhabitants (Pringle, 1834, p. 68). There they will live "Like our brave Scottish sires in the blithe Olden Day" – tending their flocks, milking their cows, and growing "rich in the wealth which a bountiful soil / Pours forth to repay the glad husbandman's toil" (p. 68). This fantasy of a fruitful wilderness, common to emigrant writing at least since the seventeenth century (Fender, 1992), concludes with the prophecy that "love's Olive plants round our table shall rise, Engrafted with hopes that bear fruit in the skies" (Pringle, 1834, p. 68). This poem presents emigration as an opportunity to reconstruct traditional ways of life – in this case the cotter's subsistence agriculture – in a new setting. In an allusion to Romans 9–11, it also acknowledges the necessity of "grafting" the wild and the cultivated, the new and the old.

This fantasy of Scottish settler domesticity does not account for the depopulation of the land that had to occur before the poet could build his beehive home. Scottish dispossession and emigration enabled the settlement of the Cape, but it also found an uncanny double in the forced migration of South Africa's Indigenous peoples. Elsewhere Pringle recognizes this connection, drawing an analogy between Highlanders cleared from their homes and dispossessed San people or "Bushmen," when he refers to the latter as "Children of the Mist," the name Walter Scott gave to Clan MacGregor in *Rob Roy* (1817) and *A Legend of Montrose* (1819). Evicted from their ancestral land, the MacGregors have become peripatetic outlaws, "a small sept of banditti, called, from their houseless state and their incessantly wandering among the mountains and glens, the Children of the Mist. They are a fierce and hardy people, with all the irritability, and wild and vengeful passions, proper to men who have never known the restraint of civilized society" (Scott, 1830, p. 102). Similarly, Pringle explains, the San

> have by the incessant encroachments of the colonists been either driven to the sterile deserts, and of necessity transformed into Bushmen, or utterly extirpated. This process has been carrying on, as the authentic records of the Colony prove, for at least a hundred and twenty years. And thus on the outskirts of our ever-advancing frontier, numerous wandering hordes of destitute and desperate savages – the South African "Children of the Mist" – have been constantly found in a state of precarious truce, or bitter hostility with the colonists. (Pringle, 1834, p. 366)

Pringle acknowledges, as Scott perhaps does not in the case of the MacGregors, that the South African Children of the Mist have been "transformed" by the experience of dispossession and that their "fierce, suspicious, and vindictive" (p. 366) ways are a response to the encroachment of settlers rather than innate traits "proper to men who have never known the restraints of civilized society."

Lara Atkin has argued that Pringle's comparison of the Scottish and South African Children of the Mist is intended "to draw an analogy between the painful integration of Scotland's Highlanders into the Anglo-Empire in the late-eighteenth century and the plight of the Cape Colony's Indigenous peoples, who were playing out a similar struggle against the expanding British colonial state in 1830s southern Africa" (2018, p. 201). Yet the analogy seems rather to call into question the possibility of such integration, and to illustrate a knock-on effect between Scottish emigration and the forced migration of South African Indigenous peoples. The Highland Clearances are an uncanny presence in *African Sketches*, rendering the forced migrations of the Cape's Indigenous peoples eerily familiar and illuminating Pringle's doubleness as dispossessed emigrant and colonial settler.

The Scottish uncanny also surfaces in "Evening Rambles," a poem indebted to the eighteenth-century prospect poetry tradition, in which Pringle finds reminders of Scotland's landscapes in his unfamiliar South African surroundings. In British prospect poetry, the landscape usually mediates between present and past; however, in a settler colonial context such as South Africa, "the past is the domain of the Other and history is the history of dispossession" (Bunn, 2002, p. 143). In settler colonial prospect poetry, therefore, the landscape instead tends to mediate between "the lost metropolitan home and the uncoded Otherness of the present" (p. 138). The landscape of the poet's own past becomes visible in the prospect before him, overwriting any evidence of a precolonial history. Thus, as he rambles, Pringle describes a picturesque landscape that "seems to tell / of primrose tufts in Scottish dell" until we "raise the eye to range / O'er prospects wild, grotesque, and strange" (Pringle, 1834, p. 21). The "sterile mountains" (p. 21) disrupt the likeness to the Scottish borders that Pringle finds in the "dusky vale," with its "homeward herds and flocks" (p. 25). As the sheep and cattle approach, the illusion is again broken, for as

> The Brown Herder with his flock
> Comes winding round my hermit-rock
> His mien and gait and vesture tell,
> No shepherd he from Scottish fell,
> For crook the guardian gun he bears,
> For plaid the sheepskin mantle wears;
> Sauntering languidly along,
> No flute has he nor merry song,
> Nor book, nor tale, nor rustic lay,
> To cheer him through his listless day.
> His look is dull, his soul is dark;
> He feels not hope's electric spark;
> But born to the White Man's servile thrall,
> Knows that he cannot lower fall. (pp. 25–26)

This stanza is worth quoting in full because it attributes the long list of differences between the Scottish shepherd and the "Brown Herder" to the latter's indentured servitude. The herder's initial uncanny evocation of a Scottish shepherd is undercut by both his attire and the intellectual vacuity and demoralization written on his countenance. Pringle not only denies the herder any "rival music" or "oral tradition" comparable to the Scottish shepherd's book and pipe, as Bunn has pointed out (2002, p. 159), but also any interiority. Pringle's notes identify the herder as a "Hottentot" or KhoiKhoi, a nomadic pastoral people driven off their land and indentured first to the Dutch and later to the British.

These indentured servants were kept "in a more degraded condition than the slaves," he explains (Pringle, 1834, p. 391).

With his "merry song" and "rustic lay," the Scottish shepherd of "Evening Rambles" belongs to both the pastoral and the past. Sheep farming was a precarious way of life in Scotland during the years following the Napoleonic Wars, when the number of shepherds dwindled (Bunn, 2002, p. 161). But if the carefree shepherd belonged to Scotland's past, he also symbolized for Pringle a possible future for South African Indigenous peoples. At the Cape, the introduction of sheep farming, the very practice that displaced so many cotters in Scotland, provided a new form of employment for displaced Indigenous peoples (p. 161). Already the "stout Neat-herd," with his "bolder step and blither eye" represents an improvement on the Hottentot's condition (Pringle, 1834, p. 26):

> From the destroying foeman fled,
> He serves the Colonist for bread:
> Yet this poor heathen Bechuan
> Bears on his brow the port of man;
> A naked, homeless exile he –
> But not debased by slavery. (p. 26)

By using the archaic term "Neat" instead of the modern "cattle," Pringle emphasizes the unimproved state of the "poor heathen Bechuan." Yet the cattle herder is less wretched than the Hottentot shepherd because he is neither an indentured servant nor a slave, but works "for bread." In his *Narrative of a Residence in South Africa*, Pringle recounts the arrival in Graff-Reinét of "several hundred . . . Bechuanas . . . driven into the colony from the northeast," whence they had fled the encroachments of "wandering hordes" of *Bergenaars*, or "bands of banditti, of mixed colonial and African lineage" (1834, pp. 359–360). To prevent these "unfortunate refugees from being reduced to a state of absolute and unconditional slavery," Pringle explains, the Bechuanas were "apprenticed out, upon certain conditions as to good treatment, among such of the colonists as did not possess slaves" (p. 360). As he recounts in his poem the "The Bechuana Boy," Pringle and his wife took in one of the displaced Bechuanas "for 'our own'" (p. 8). The phrase "our own," which Pringle sets off in quotation marks, signals the uncomfortable proximity of the apprenticed Bechuanas to enslaved peoples.

In "The Bechuana Boy," the settler domesticity celebrated in "The Emigrant's Song," "The Emigrant's Cabin," and others of Pringle's South African poems, becomes a paradigm of what Angus Calder calls Pringle's humanitarian Christian colonialism (1982, p. 3) – his belief that the teachings of Christianity modeled by British settlers would civilize the native peoples of South Africa and raise them above the indigence or slavery to which they had been reduced. The poem recounts the sudden appearance of a "swarthy Stripling" and his "tame Springbok" while Pringle is riding in the desert (Pringle, 1834, p. 1). The boy explains that he has "no home": his village was burned by the Bergenaars, its men were killed, and its women and children were driven across "the dreary wild" to be sold at a slave market (pp. 2, 3). Bought by a Dutch farmer, the boy has endured "Harsh blows, and scorn, and shame," all of which he could have withstood had he "but found a single friend" (pp. 4, 5). His longing for a companion is fulfilled when he rescues a wounded springbok and "nurse[s] it in a cavern wild / Until it loved me like a child" (p. 6). The parallels between the boy and his four-legged companion are difficult to miss: while the boy's village is set upon by a "relentless robber clan," the springbok's herd is chased by "wolfish wild-dogs," and both are left alone and bereft (pp. 2, 6). They are further alike in their meek and docile dispositions. When Pringle first encounters them, the boy is "Caressing with a gentle hand / That beast of gentle brood," a Blakean tableau that emphasizes their mutual affection and, for want of a better word, their tameness (p. 2). The boy with his "open aspect" and "modest mien" is no more an uncivilized savage than the pet springbok is a wild animal (p. 2). He begs Pringle, "let me serve thee, as thine own, / For I am in the world alone!" (pp. 7, 8).

The boy's docility enables his assimilation as a servant into Pringle's household. Matthew Shum (2009) has analyzed the similarities between the story of Marossi, the Bechuana child whom the Pringles adopted, and Mary Prince: both, by Pringle's account, voluntarily offered themselves up as a servant to him, seeking his benevolent paternal protection. Marossi's story follows a similar trajectory to Prince's, beginning with the traumatic disruption of family life, followed by a descent into the horrors of slavery, and concluding with rescue and religious rehabilitation as the Pringles' servant. The last stanza of "The Bechuana Boy" describes the transformations necessary for Marossi's successful integration into the Pringles' domestic circle:

> Such was Marossi's touching tale.
> Our breasts they were not made of stone:
> His words, his winning looks prevail –
> We took him for "our own."
> And One, with woman's gentle art,
> Unlocked the fountains of his heart:
> And love gushed forth – till he became
> Her Child in every thing but name. (Pringle, 1834, p. 8)

The boy's rehabilitation depends both on his ability to appeal to the Pringles' sensibilities with his "touching tale" and on Mrs. Pringle's ability to further refine a nature that Pringle describes in his note to the poem as "singularly

ingenuous and affectionate" (p. 501). Similarly, Prince must couch her autobiography in terms that will win her English readership's sympathy in order to
prove herself worthy of the freedom she desires.

The incorporation of Marossi – and arguably also Prince – into the
Pringles' household models in miniature Pringle's vision of a benevolent
colonialism. Pringle sums up this vision toward the end of his narrative
when he urges, "Let us subdue savage Africa by JUSTICE, by KINDNESS,
by the talisman of CHRISTIAN TRUTH. Let us thus go forth in the name
and under the blessing of God, gradually to extend the moral influence, and
if it be thought desirable, the territorial boundary of our Colony until it shall
become an Empire" (Pringle, 1834, pp. 479–480). This triumphalist passage
demonstrates that Pringle's antislavery stance was not simply compatible
with but also arguably dependent upon an evangelical form of British
imperial rule. It also sheds light on Mary Prince's experiences in "the service
of Mr and Mrs Pringle," where, Prince relates, "My mistress teaches me
daily to read the word of God, and takes great pains to make me understand
it" (2000, p. 36). Pringle's wife becomes the instrument of domestic colonialism for both Marossi and Prince, as she imparts the religious instruction
that will "subdue [the] savage." The teachings of Christianity prepared
Prince, in the Pringles' eyes, for the freedom they sought for her, and
these teachings also consigned her to a state of servitude while she awaited
the resolution of her fate.

While Pringle's life experiences clearly illustrate the interconnections
between dwelling and depopulation in Scotland and South Africa, his representations of the relationship between dispossession and domesticity in
African Sketches are more ambiguous. On one hand, the displacement of
South African Indigenous peoples finds its uncanny double in the agricultural
transformations that forced Scottish cotters from their homes. On the other
hand, Scottish settler colonial domesticity reconstructed in a new land the
pious affections and patriarchal order of Burns's cotter family, absorbing into
its embrace those dispossessed peoples who demonstrated their improvabil-
ity. Although Pringle was troubled by the dispossession and enslavement of
South African Indigenous peoples under British colonial rule, the understanding of racial difference that he inherited from the Scottish
Enlightenment precluded him from considering the protection of their traditional ways of life as a desirable option. Pringle's time at the Cape informed
his abhorrence of slavery and his tireless work to abolish it, but it also
informed his vision of a humanitarian Christian imperialism that would
gently and with the best of intentions accomplish the same ends as the
violence and injustice he condemned.

4.2 Providence and the Female Emigrant

Strickland Moodie's conversion to Methodism and her introduction to Thomas Pringle led both to the abolitionist awakening that she describes in the preface to Ashton Warner's *Negro Slavery Described by a Negro* and to her literary reformation – her determination to use her talents as an author for higher purposes than mere entertainment. We might expect to find her experiences as Prince's amanuensis leave a lasting mark on her work; indeed, some of the stories she wrote in the early 1830s do refute racial prejudices, depicting Black characters as worthy of readers' sympathies. That her concern with combatting prejudice peters out quite quickly may reflect Strickland Moodie's belief that with the Slavery Abolition Act of 1833 her work was done. Yet echoes of Prince's *History* reverberate in Strickland Moodie's struggle to find spiritual meaning and providential design in the trials of emigration and settlement. Emigration was a traumatic event for Strickland Moodie, and her compulsive recounting of stories of emigration, beginning even before she left England, suggests that she never really came to terms with separation from the country of her birth. Early iterations of these stories register Strickland Moodie's awareness of the deleterious effects of British emigration on Indigenous peoples in the colonies and find revelations of providential design in settlers' interactions with them. But later versions share Prince's skepticism that any divine plan underlies the exile's sufferings. By the time she came to publish *Roughing It*, the experiences of Black and Indigenous peoples have been displaced to the margins of her narrative.

"The Vanquished Lion," first published in *Ackermann's Juvenile Forget Me Not: A Christmas, New Year's and Birth-Day Present for 1832* (1831), is the earliest version of a story about emigration that Strickland Moodie would retell repeatedly over the next two decades. It must have been written several months after the publication of Prince's *History* at a time when Strickland Moodie and her husband were discussing their own departure from England and the possibility of settling in South Africa. "The Vanquished Lion" tells the story of the Fenwick family's emigration to the Cape after an unspecified misfortune has left them "unable to maintain a genteel appearance in England" (1991, p. 32). Young Lewis Fenwick looks forward to seeing the exotic wildlife and vegetation described by "Mr. Pringle . . . in his beautiful poem" (p. 32), but his mother finds it "very hard to bear" the prospect of leaving a "happy home, and . . . dear friends" (p. 32). She is speaking to herself more than to Lewis when she reminds him that "God, my dear child, has appointed the future; and it is weak and sinful in short-sighted mortals like us to murmur at his will. To submit with cheerfulness to the dispensations of Providence is to overcome the world, and to disarm sorrow of its sting" (p. 32). Strong in her belief that Providence has ordained the family's emigration, Mrs. Fenwick nonetheless struggles to resign herself to this divine plan, against which her pride, associated here with "the world," rebels.

Despite having read Pringle's "Afar in the Desert" and George Thompson's *Travels and Adventures in Southern Africa* (1827), young Lewis is unprepared for his initial encounter with Black people. Upon the family's arrival at the Cape, "Lewis felt the prejudices of colour operating very forcibly upon his mind against the natives of the country, which from this period, he was to consider his own" (Strickland Moodie, 1991, p. 36), and he cannot be persuaded to talk to Charka, the "dark-skinned escort" who guides them from the coast to the interior (p. 36). Mrs. Fenwick points out to her son the absurdity of "regard[ing] with aversion a fellow-creature, whom God has endowed with rational faculties and feelings as keen as your own, merely because his skin is of a different hue" (pp. 36–37). Prejudice, she implies, may be an instinctive reaction to the unfamiliar, but it has no basis in reason and thus should be susceptible to logical argument. Those who keep slaves, such as Lewis's uncle and Charka's master, Mr. Clayton, "have never rightly considered the subject" and unthinkingly follow "the customs of the land" (p. 37). When Lewis learns that Charka is enslaved, he is "sorry for him" and regrets his initial "hatred and disgust" (p. 37). But it is not until Charka saves Lewis's life by killing a snake that has wound itself around the sleeping boy that Lewis develops "a most tender and grateful attachment" to Charka (p. 40). Lewis beseeches his uncle to repay Charka's "great kindness" in saving his life by freeing him, declaring his belief "that it is impossible for any man to be happy whilst he remains a slave!" (p. 40). Schooled by his nephew's example, Mr. Clayton determines "to emancipate every slave" he owns (p. 40).

The freeing of Charka would seem a natural place for the story to end, as Lewis has overcome his prejudice and demonstrated his understanding that Charka is a human being entitled to the same liberties that he himself enjoys. But Mrs. Fenwick's struggles to resign herself to the will of God remain unresolved until Lewis's younger brother Arthur is also subjected to a near-death experience, an encounter with a lion. When Mrs. Fenwick sees the beast pawing her child, she utters "one brief prayer to the Father of Mercies to protect her from evil, and . . . flinging herself on her knees before the majestic animal, she snatched the child" away from it (Strickland Moodie, 1991, p. 42). The lion represents not only the dangers that threaten settlers far from the safety of civilization but also the worldly pride that Mrs. Fenwick must vanquish in order to reconcile herself to her reduced circumstances. The animal's release of Arthur indicates that "the mother's prayer had been heard" (pp. 41–42) and that her struggles have been sanctified.

"The Vanquished Lion" reveals Moodie's understanding of the causal connections between British emigration and settlement and the dispossession and enslavement of Indigenous peoples. Yet, as the title of the story suggests, the focus of "The Vanquished Lion" for Strickland Moodie is not Charka's liberation, but rather Mrs. Fenwick's conquest of her rebellious feelings and her resignation to God's will. The plight of Indigenous peoples becomes increasingly peripheral to later versions of this story, as Strickland Moodie becomes more concerned with affirming, and perhaps with reassuring herself, that the emigrant's experiences are part of a divine scheme even if they seem to reflect the glaring absence of any providential care. "The Broken Mirror. A True Tale," published in the *Literary Garland* in 1843, tells another version of the emigrant's providential salvation through Indigenous intermediaries. When Mrs. Harden, wife of an Edinburgh merchant, is suddenly widowed, she and her two sons decide to emigrate to the Cape in the hope of repairing their fortunes. All their property must be sold to pay their debts, but Mrs. Harden, "a weak, erring woman, still too much in love with the world" (Strickland Moodie, 1991, p. 72), insists on keeping a Turkish rug and an Italian mirror, which, with much difficulty, she transports to the Cape. When the ship is unloaded, the mirror is found broken and the rug soaked with salt water so that its colors have run.

Misao Dean reads the shattering of the mirror as "the rupture in the ideology of the feminine which results from the voyage, both mental and physical, from Briton to colonist" (1998, p. 29). Having lost wealth, status, and home, Mrs. Harden must confront once again "the instability of earthly riches" with the breaking of the mirror that once reflected a coherent feminine identity. Her son Robert insists on taking the spoiled goods to the frontier anyway, saying "Such is my trust in God, that I believe He is able to turn these broken fragments, that you despise, to good account" (Strickland Moodie, 1991, p. 80). And he is proven right when the natives barter "flocks of sheep and herds of cattle for these once despised fragments of broken glass" in which they can admire their own "sable visages" (p. 83). The soiled carpet is made into colorful garments that "had as great a sale as the pieces of glass" (p. 84). Robert rejoices that "God has restored to us the value of the mirror seven-fold! Who will ever doubt his providential care, who listens to the tale of our Broken Mirror" (p. 84). Mrs. Harden's clinging to the remnants of her worldly goods is justified and even rewarded as "from being the poorest and most dependent settlers in the glen, the widow and her sons became the most wealthy and independent" (p. 84). The Harden family's prosperity is built on the feminine tendencies of the "savage chiefs" to delight in gazing at their own features (p. 83). Mrs. Harden's vanity and attachment to material possessions that, unlike cows and sheep, have little intrinsic value are at once validated and ridiculed by the similar propensities of Indigenous peoples.

Setting her stories at the Cape allowed Strickland Moodie to explore her anxieties about emigration in a displaced setting, one that she had rejected because of both her fear of wild animals and her dislike of slavery. While Canada possessed both of these evils – the latter nominally only until 1834 – Strickland Moodie believed them to be less pervasive there than in South Africa. "The Broken Mirror" is a fantasy of wish fulfillment that configures settlers' struggles for material prosperity as a spiritual endeavor, so that worldly wealth acquired through hard work and faith in God becomes a sign of salvation, and faith in God in turn brings the promise of worldly wealth. It is difficult, then, to know what to make of "The Well in the Wilderness" (1847), the only one of Strickland Moodie's stories set in North America. Published in the first issue of *Victoria Magazine*, a short-lived periodical run by Strickland Moodie and her husband, its grim portrayal of emigration suggests that even after fifteen years in Canada, she was still reliving the trauma of separation from her homeland. The story's gruesome ending, a rewriting of "The Vanquished Lion," indicates the strain of attempting to preserve English ideals of femininity in settler colonial conditions.

"The Well in the Wilderness" reflects Strickland Moodie's belief that "women ... feel parting with the old familiar places and faces, more keenly than men" (1991, p. 90). Like Mrs. Fenwick in "The Vanquished Lion," Mrs. Steele's attachment to her home in "The Well in the Wilderness" renders emigration, in Dean's words, "almost physically debilitating" (1998, p. 31). But when her husband finds that "labor in his native land, could no longer give his children bread," Mrs. Steele, a model of uxorial obedience, "made no opposition" to his insistence that they emigrate (Strickland Moodie, 1991, p. 89). Her deference to her husband's authority despite her misgivings demonstrates the endurance and self-denial that, as Dean notes, are essential qualities of settler colonial femininity for Strickland Moodie. Mrs. Steele's deference to her husband also reflects her obedience to a higher patriarchal authority, a "perfect and childlike reliance upon God" (p. 91). Yet Mrs. Steele's faith seems misplaced, for, in contrast to Mrs. Fenwick and Mrs. Harden, her resignation to the will of Providence is not rewarded. The Steeles settle in Illinois at the edge of a dark forest that surrounds the nearest well, and when the children fall ill with the ague, Mrs. Steele must venture into the forest alone to fetch them water. When, hours later, Mr. Steele sets out in search of his wife, he hears "a low deep growling, and the crunching of teeth, as if some wild animal was devouring the bones of its prey" and stumbles across her "disfigured and mutilated body," which has been partially eaten by a panther (p. 97).

Mrs. Steele's horrible death enacts Strickland Moodie's fears of the dangers of the wilderness. In *Roughing It*, Moodie describes herself as "haunted with visions of wolves and bears," confessing that when walking alone, "Often have I stopped and reproached myself for want of faith in the goodness of Providence, and repeated the text, 'The wicked are afraid when no man pursueth: but the righteous are as bold as a lion,' as if to shame myself into courage" (2007, p. 184). Even more frightening than predatory animals is the possibility suggested by Mrs. Steele's death that there may be no benevolent God watching over emigrants and no spiritual meaning in their trials. If Mrs. Steele's death is meaningless, so, it seems, was her life. Although she is not forgotten, "time as it ever does, softened the deep anguish" of her husband and children, and many years later, after "the little settlement" has become "a prosperous village . . . Richard Steele died a wealthy man" (Strickland Moodie, 1991, p. 97). It is difficult not to feel that Mr. Steele is slightly callous, first in tearing his wife from her beloved birthplace, and subsequently in remaining – and apparently thriving – at the site of such a calamity.

Roughing It was the culmination of Strickland Moodie's various retellings of the story of her emigration, and it replaces the imagined Indigenous peoples of her earlier fiction with portrayals of the Native peoples she actually encountered in Upper Canada. Critics have commented on the absence of Black people in *Roughing It* (Whitlock, 2000, p. 61; Medovarski, 2014), which is remarkable even though the narrative was largely written before the passage of the Fugitive Slave Act in the United States in 1850 sent an influx of Black settlers to Canada, doubling the Black population of Ontario in a decade (Siemerling 2015, p. 86). However, Strickland Moodie does register the earlier presence of Blacks in Canada when she relates the story of Tom Smith, a fugitive slave killed in a charivari after marrying an Irishwoman (2007, p. 140). However, she is less concerned with championing Smith's marriage than with condemning those who expressed their disapprobation of it so violently. This episode thus illustrates Gillian Whitlock's claim that uneducated, lower-class white settlers rather than Black or Indigenous peoples play the part of the racial "other" in *Roughing It* (2000, p. 66).

Indeed, Strickland Moodie expresses admiration for and affinity with Native peoples, to whom she attributes an innate dignity, because they are at once more obviously different and less threateningly so than the uneducated Irish and Scottish rabble who carouse on the beaches of Grosse Isle. The Indigenous tribes' attachment to particular locales recalls her own deep affection for the landscape of her childhood home. In describing a "dry cedar-swamp" near their house in the bush, Strickland Moodie notes that it had been the Ojibway people's "usual place of encampment for many years," and that "although the favourite spot had now passed into the hands of strangers, they still frequented the place" (2007, p. 187). Similarly, she observes that Native peoples depend "for their subsistence" upon the small islands dotting the lake by her house and are "very jealous of the settlers in the country coming to hunt and fish here" (p. 228). It does not seem to occur to Strickland Moodie that she is among the "strangers" who had seized this favored land or one of the intrusive settlers whose presence the Indigenous peoples resent. Instead, she naturalizes the displacement of the Ojibway from their hereditary land by representing it as part of an inscrutable providential plan, as evidence of divine schema that she cannot discern in her own experiences of migration. When she remarks "that a mysterious destiny involves and hangs over them, pressing them back into the wilderness, and slowly and surely sweeping them from the earth" (p. 200), Strickland Moodie creates her own version of the American doctrine of Manifest Destiny, in which British settlement wears the guise of "mysterious destiny."

Despite her analysis of the Ojibways' fate, Strickland Moodie ultimately abandoned the belief that her own emigration was part of a divinely ordained plan. When the family moved from their first settlement near Cobourg further into the backwoods, Strickland Moodie combated a "foreboding sadness" by recalling that what brought her to Canada was "Providence":

> Not for your own welfare, perhaps, but for the welfare of your children, the unerring hand of the Great Father has led you here. You form a connecting link in the destinies of many. It is impossible for any human creature to live for himself alone. It may be your lot to suffer, but others will reap a benefit from your trials. (2007, p. 178)

According to Strickland Moodie's logic, her renunciation of the comforts of civilization and self-sacrificial resignation to God's will should entail material rewards, if not for herself then for future generations. By the time she came to write the preface to *Roughing It*, however, Strickland Moodie concluded that it was not through "the middle ranks of British society . . . that Providence works when it would reclaim the waste places of the earth" (2007, p. 11) – presumably the very "waste places" from which the Ojibway had been swept. The tribulations her family experienced in their first seven years in Canada – illness, poverty, crop failure, and fire, among others – must have led Strickland Moodie to question both her ability to divine the ways of Providence and the wisdom of the decision to emigrate.

The series of stories that Strickland Moodie wrote about migration suggests that if her encounter with Mary Prince did have a lasting impact on her work, it was less in awakening her consciousness of the evils of slavery than in establishing her sympathy with Prince's feelings at the end of her *History* when she describes it as "a hard and heavy task" to believe that God "knows what is good for me better than I know myself" (2000, p. 37). Although her sufferings were lighter, Strickland Moodie too found it difficult to believe the isolation and frustration she experienced as an emigrant were part of a providential plan. The only time after 1831 that Strickland Moodie mentions Prince is, perhaps unsurprisingly, in one of her many retellings of the story of her emigration. In 1851, she acknowledged her role in recording Prince's narrative in "Trifles from the Burthen of a Life," first published in the *Literary Garland* and subsequently expanded into a novel, *Flora Lyndsay* (1854). These two works constitute prequels to *Roughing It*, describing preparations for emigration and the voyage to Canada. On a vessel sailing from the south of England to Edinburgh, from whence she will depart for Canada, Rachel, the protagonist of "Trifles," meets on board a "young negro lad" who shocks the passengers with his brash antics (Strickland Moodie, 1991, p. 217). His enslaver, Mrs. Dalton, claims that the Black boy's "pertness" is "the effect of the stir made by the English people against slavery," and mentions in particular *The History of Mary Prince* as a "canting tract" and "an imaginary tale, got up for party purposes" (p. 228). Rachel retorts that she knows the "narrative to be strictly true, for I took it down myself from the woman's own lips" (p. 228) and condemns slavery as "a system of injustice and cruelty that is a disgrace to a Christian community" (p. 228).

Why did Strickland Moodie choose to describe this encounter – which may or may not have occurred in fact – twenty years after the publication of *The History of Mary Prince*? Did she feel that she been unfairly deprived of recognition for her role in producing Prince's *History*? Did she regret that, in the aftermath of the *History*'s publication, she had not insisted upon the truth of Prince's narrative as Rachel does here? Or was she simply reliving a moment when she felt a sense of purpose and agency that she had long since lost? Whatever the reason, its place in the story of her emigration suggests that the recording of Prince's narrative was a formative moment in Strickland Moodie's life, one involved in several significant transitions – from young woman to wife and mother, emigrant to immigrant, enthusiastic Briton to reluctant Canadian. The transatlantic voyage that took Strickland Moodie to Canada opened up a chasm in her life, separating her from her past life as much as if, in her own words, "the grave had closed over" her (2007, p. 82). Prince belonged on the other side of the chasm, to life beyond the grave.

5 Conclusion: Afterlives

Mary Prince, Thomas Pringle, and Susanna Strickland Moodie have acquired the status of founding figures in, respectively, Caribbean, South African, and Canadian literary traditions. But they also reveal the limitations of the national traditions within which scholars have placed them. Prince has been claimed as a canonical figure in British Romantic and Black British writing, while Strickland Moodie and Pringle have become divorced from their pre-settler-colonial pasts as British writers. In part because of their problematic relation-ships to national literary traditions, Prince, Pringle, and Strickland Moodie continue to fascinate writers working at the intersection of the Black and Anglophone Atlantic worlds. Although all three left autobiographical narra-tives, they remain enigmatic figures, offering tantalizing insights into experi-ences that are ultimately perhaps incommunicable.

Prince, the most enigmatic, is the subject of Caribbean-American writer Gale Jackson's poem "mary prince: bermuda. turks island. antigua. 1787," the final stanza of which evokes both the inconclusiveness of Prince's *History* and its foundational status in Black Atlantic writing:

> god knows what's in store
> from here on
> but when they tell the story
> they gots to begin with mine. (1992, p. 8)

Prince's narrative marks an origin point for the Black diasporic women's literary tradition to which Jackson herself contributes. The open-endedness of the story of Black women's exploitation leaves it up to readers to determine "what's in store from here on," or what they will do with what they have learned from Prince.

Margaret Atwood's *The Journals of Susanna Moodie*, a series of poems written in Moodie's voice, similarly takes *Roughing It* as a foundational Canadian text, exploring the self-division that permeates Strickland Moodie's writing and that Atwood sees as characteristic of the Canadian condition. In "Thoughts from Underground," this self-division infects the form of the poem, as Moodie, speaking from her grave, recalls:

> I felt I ought to love
> this country.
>   I said I loved it
> and my mind saw double.
>
> I began to forget myself
> in the middle
> of sentences. Events
> Were split apart. (1970, pp. 54–55)

The enjambment of short sentences across lines and stanzas reflects the splitting apart of Moodie's psyche and the emergence of the "violent duality" of embrace and exile (p. 62).

Dionne Brand's autobiographical *A Map to the Door of No Return* (2002) complicates the doubleness that Atwood understands as central to Canadian identity by restoring *The History of Mary Prince*, repressed and all but disavowed by Moodie, as a competing source text for that identity. Andrea Medovarski argues that *A Map to the Door of No Return* "might be read as a twenty-first century manifestation of the ways Susanna Moodie's Canadian landscape is haunted by Mary Prince's Caribbean one," as it intertwines descriptions of Brand's life in the Canadian backwoods with memories of her Caribbean childhood: "The snow and trees of the Canadian North are reflected through the waves of the sea; the forty-fifth parallel collides with the tenth" (2014, pp. 143, 152). *A Map to the Door of No Return* foregrounds the dependence of settler colonial societies in the Anglophone Atlantic world on the Black Atlantic – that is, on slavery – and of settler colonial literatures on the suppression of Black stories.

Thomas Pringle, although a very minor figure in Scottish and British Romantic literary histories, enjoys an afterlife as the problematically paternalistic adoptive "father" of South African poetry. He haunts *The One That Got Away* (2009), a collection of short stories by Zoë Wicomb, a South African-born writer who has lived for much of her adult life in Scotland, reversing the trajectory of Pringle's own migration. In "Disgrace," a story that alludes to J. M. Coetzee's novel of the same name, Glaswegian writer Fiona McAllister visits South Africa, where her research on Thomas Pringle becomes entangled in her own creative and political self-definition in ways that cringingly replicate Pringle's benevolent imperialism. The story, set immediately following the end of apartheid, suggests that the legacies of settler colonial ideologies cannot easily be erased.

If Prince, Strickland Moodie, and Pringle individually continue to influence writers across the Atlantic world, their collaboration also has its successors in projects that aim to bring to metropolitan readers the stories of the dispossessed. One striking example of this is *Refugee Tales*, a series of books published in collaboration with a prestigious group of British writers including Jackie Kay, Ali Smith, Bernadine Evaristo, and Monica Ali. Under current law, the UK can detain immigrants indefinitely before they are either deported – sent back to countries where their lives may be in danger – or provisionally admitted. During this time, they cannot work or begin to build a community in the country where they have sought asylum. The UK pressure group Detention Action has found that "In 2020 Black people are detained in wildly disproportionate numbers and for longer periods than white people" (Townsend 2020). *Refugee Tales* brings public attention to the dehumanizing treatment that these detainees endure, but these volumes do not pretend to offer unmediated, verbatim records of the detainees' accounts. Instead, inspired by *The Canterbury Tales*, a foundational text that describes a pilgrimage of a different sort, it aims to honor them by making them into literature, acknowledging and even foregrounding the mediation of the original accounts. This project raises important questions about whose words literary scholars value and under what conditions – when and of whom we demand authenticity and when we seek literariness. The ethical and literary questions raised by the publication of *The History of Mary Prince* are far from resolved today.

References

Aljoe, Nicole N. (2014). Introduction: Remapping the Early Slave Narrative. In Nicole N. Aljoe and Ian Finseth, eds., *Journeys of the Slave Narrative in the Early Americas*. Charlottesville: University of Virginia Press, pp. 1–16.

Allen, Jessica L. (2012). Pringle's Pruning of Prince: *The History of Mary Prince* and the Question of Repetition. *Callaloo*, 35(2), 509–519.

[Anon.]. (1831). The Anti-Slavery Society and the West India Colonists. *Bermuda Royal Gazette*, 47(4), 1.

Atkin, Lara. (2018). The South African "Children of the Mist": The Bushman, the Highlander and the Making of Colonial Identities in Thomas Pringle's South African Poetry (1825–1834). *Yearbook of English Studies*, 48, 199–215.

Atwood, Margaret. (1970). *The Journals of Susanna Moodie*. Toronto: Oxford University Press.

Ballantyne, Tony. (2007). What Difference Does Colonialism Make? Reassessing Print and Social Change in an Age of Global Imperialism. In Sabrina Alcorn Baron, Eric N. Lindquist, and Eleanor F. Shevlin, eds., *Agent of Change: Print Culture Studies after Elizabeth L. Eisenstein*. Amherst: University of Massachusetts Press, pp. 342–352.

Ballstadt, Carl. (1965). The Literary History of the Strickland Family. DPhilThesis, University of London.

Ballstadt, Carl, Elizabeth Hopkins, and Michael Peterman, eds. (1985). *Letters of a Lifetime*. Toronto: University of Toronto Press.

Banner, Rachel. (2013). Surface and Stasis: Re-reading Slave Narrative via *The History of Mary Prince*. *Callaloo*, 36(2), 298–311.

Baumgartner, Barbara. (2001). The Body As Evidence: Resistance, Collaboration, and Appropriation in *The History of Mary Prince*. *Callaloo*, 24(1), 253–275.

Belich, James. (2009). *Replenishing the Earth: The Settler Revolution and the Rise of the Anglo-World, 1783–1939*. Oxford: Oxford University Press.

Bird, William Wilberforce. (1823). *The State of the Cape of Good Hope in 1822, by a Civil Servant of the Colony*. London: John Murray.

Bland, Sterling L. (1990). *Voices of the Fugitives: Runaway Slave Stories and Their Fictions of Self-Creation*. Westport, CT: Greenwood Press.

Bohls, Elizabeth A. (2014). *Slavery and the Politics of Place: Representing the Colonial Caribbean, 1770–1833*. Cambridge: Cambridge University Press.

Briggs, Charles Frederick. (1852). Preface. In *Roughing It in the Bush*, by Susanna Strickland Moodie. New York: George Putnam, pp. ii–iii.

Bunn, David. (2002). "Our Wattled Cot": Mercantile and Domestic Space in Thomas Pringle's African Landscapes. In W. J. T. Mitchell, ed., *Landscape and Power*, 2nd ed. Chicago:University of Chicago Press, pp. 127–173.

Calder, Angus. (1982). Thomas Pringle (1789–1834): A Scottish Poet in South Africa. *English in Africa*, 9(1), 1–13.

Caretta, Vincent. (2003). Introduction. In *Unchained Voices: An Anthology of Black Voices in the English-Speaking World of the Eighteenth Century.* Lexington: University of Kentucky Press, pp. 1–16.

Carey, Brycchan. (2005). *British Abolitionism and the Rhetoric of Sensibility: Writing, Sentiment and Slavery, 1760–1804.* New York: Palgrave Macmillan.

Cave, Roderick. (1978). Early Printing and the Book Trade in the West Indies. *Library Quarterly*, 48(2), 163–192.

Clarke, George Elliott. (2005). This Is No Hearsay: Reading the Canadian Slave Narrative. *Papers of the Bibliographical Society of Canada*, 43(1), 7–32.

Collier, Patrick, and James T. Conolly. (2016). Print Culture Histories beyond the Metropolis: An Introduction. In James T. Connolly, Patrick Collier, Frank Felsenstein, Kenneth Hall, and Robert G. Hall, eds., *Print Culture Histories beyond the Metropolis*. Toronto: University of Toronto Press, pp. 3–25.

Davies, Carole Boyce. (2002). *Black Women, Writing and Identity: Migrations of the Subject*, 2nd ed. New York: Routledge.

Dean, Misao. (1992). Concealing Her Bluestockings: Femininity and Self-Representation in Susanna Moodie's Autobiographical Works. In Gillian Whitlock and Helen Tiffin, eds., *Re-siting Queen's English: Text and Tradition in Postcolonial Literature*. Amsterdam:Rodopoi, pp. 25–36.

(1998). *Practising Femininity: Domestic Realism and the Performance of Gender in Early Canadian Fiction*. Toronto: University of Toronto Press.

Devine, T. M. (2011). *To the Ends of the Earth: Scotland's Global Diaspora, 1750–2010*. Washington, DC: Smithsonian Books.

Ellis, Markman. (1996). *The Politics of Sensibility: Race, Gender, and Commerce in the Sentimental Novel*. Cambridge: Cambridge University Press.

Eltis, David. (2002). Introduction: Migration and Agency in Global History. In David Eltis, ed., *Coerced and Free Migration: Global Perspectives*. Stanford: Stanford University Press, pp. 1–32.

[Fairbarn, John]. (1824). On Literary and Scientific Societies. *South African Journal*, 1(1), 50–55.

Fender, Stephen. (1992). *Sea Changes: British Emigration and American Literature*. New York: Cambridge University Press.

Flynn, Philip. (2006). Beginning *Blackwood's*: The Right Mix of Dulce and Utile. *Victorian Periodicals Review*, 39(2), 136–157.

Fraser, Robert. (2008). *Book History through Postcolonial Eyes: Rewriting the Script*. London: Routledge.

Gadpaille, Michelle. (2016). Trans-colonial Collaboration and Slave Narrative: *Mary Prince* Revisited. *ELOPE: English Language Overseas Perspectives and Enquiries*, 8(2), 63–77.

Gilroy, Paul. *The Black Atlantic: Modernity and Double-Consciousness.* Cambridge, MA: Harvard University Press.

Goodman, Kevis. (2008). Romantic Poetry and the Science of Nostalgia. In James Chandler and Maureen N. McLane, eds., *The Cambridge Companion to British Romantic Poetry.* Cambridge: Cambridge University Press, pp. 195–216.

Hamilton, Douglas (2005). *Scotland, the Caribbean and the Atlantic World, 1750–1820.* Manchester: Manchester University Press.

Hanley, Ryan. (2019). *Beyond Slavery and Abolition: Black British Writing, c. 1770–1830.* Cambridge: Cambridge University Press.

Jackson, Gale. (1992). "mary prince bermuda. turks island. antigua. 1787." *Kenyon Review*, 14(1), 6–8.

Jacobs, Harriet. (2019). *Incidents in the Life of a Slave Girl*, 2nd ed., ed by Frances Smith Foster and Richard Yarborough. New York: Norton.

Kitson, Peter J. (2007). *Romantic Literature, Race and Colonial Encounter.* New York: Palgrave Macmillan.

Lambert, David. (2008). The "Glasgow King of Billingsgate": James MacQueen and the Atlantic Proslavery Network. *Slavery and Abolition*, 29(3), 389–418.

Lorimer, Douglas. (1978). *Colour, Class and the Victorians: English Attitudes to the Negro in the Mid-Nineteenth Century.* Leicester: Leicester University Press.

MacKenzie, John. (2012). *The Scots in South Africa: Ethnicity, Identity, Gender, and Race, 1772–1914.* With Nigel Dalziel. Manchester: Manchester University Press.

MacQueen, James. (1831a). Letter Fourth. To His Grace the Duke of Wellington, &c. &c. *Blackwood's Edinburgh Magazine*, 29(176), 187–213.

(1831b). British Colonies – James Stephen. Letter to the Right Honourable Earl Grey, &c. &c. &c. *Blackwood's Edinburgh Magazine*, 29(178), 454–466.

(1831c). The Colonial Empire of Great Britain. Letter to Early Grey, First Lord of the Treasury, &c. &c. *Blackwood's Edinburgh Magazine* 30(187), 744–764.

(1832). The Rev. Mr. Curtin and the Colonial Office. *Glasgow Courier*, April 21, 1.

McBride, Dwight A. (2001). *Impossible Witnesses: Truth, Abolitionism, and Slave Testimony*. New York: New York University Press.

McGann, Jerome. (1983). *The Romantic Ideology: A Critical Interpretation*. Chicago: University of Chicago Press.

McNeil, Kenneth. (2019). Diasporas: Thomas Pringle and Mary Prince. In JoEllen DeLucia and Juliet Shields, eds., *Migration and Modernities: The State of Being Stateless, 1750–1850*. Edinburgh: Edinburgh University Press, pp. 51–76.

Medovarski, Andrea. (2014). Roughing It in Bermuda: Mary Prince, Susanna Strickland Moodie, Dionne Brand, and the Black Diaspora. *Canadian Literature*, 220, 94–115.

Midgley, Claire. (1992). *Women against Slavery: The British Campaigns, 1780–1870*. London: Routledge.

Moodie, Susanna Strickland. (1831). *Enthusiasm and Other Poems*. London: Smith, Elder & Company.

(1991). *Voyages: Short Narratives of Susanna Moodie*, ed. by John Thurston. Ottawa: University of Ottawa Press.

(2007). *Roughing It in the Bush*, ed. by Michael A. Peterman. New York: Norton.

Paquet, Sandra Pouchet. (2002). *Caribbean Autobiography: Cultural Identity and Self-Representation*. Madison: University of Wisconsin Press.

Patterson, Orlando. (1982). *Slavery and Social Death: A Comparative Study*. Cambridge, MA: Harvard University Press.

Pereira, Ernest, and Michael Chapman. (1989). Introduction. In *The African Poems of Thomas Pringle*, ed. by Ernest Pereira and Michael Chapman. Pietermaritzburg: University of Natal Press, pp. i–xxviii.

Prince, Mary. (2000). *The History of Mary Prince, A West Indian Slave, Related by Herself*, ed. by Sara Salih. London: Penguin.

Pringle, Thomas. (1824a). *Some Account of the Present State of the English Settlers of Albany, South Africa*. London: T. and G. Underwood.

(1824b). Verses, On seeing in a late packet of English Papers, the Surrender of Cadiz, and the Proscription of a Free Press in Germany and Switzerland,–by Order of the "Holy Alliance." *South African Journal* 1(1), 8–9.

(1834). *African Sketches*. London: Edward Moxon.

(1966). *Narrative of a Residence in South Africa*. Cape Town: C. Struik.

Pringle, Thomas, and John Fairbarn. (1824). Prospectus. *South African Journal* 1(1), n.p.

Rauwerda, Antje M. (2001). Naming, Agency, and "A Tissue of Falsehoods" in The History of Mary Prince. *Victorian Literature and Culture*, 29(2), 397–411.

Rieley, Honor. (2016). Writing Emigration: Canada in Scottish Romanticism, 1802–1840. DPhil Thesis, University of Oxford.

Rezek, Joseph. (2015). *London and the Making of Provincial Literature*. Philadelphia: University of Pennsylvania Press.

Robertson, James. (2014). Eighteenth-Century Jamaica's Ambivalent Cosmopolitanism. *History: The Journal of the Historical Association*, 99 (337), 607–631.

Scott, Walter. (1830). *Tales of My Landlord. Third Series. The Bride of Lammermoor and A Legend of Montrose*. Boston: Samuel H. Parker.

Sharp, Sarah. (2019). Exporting "The Cotter's Saturday Night": Robert Burns, Scottish Romantic Nationalism, and Settler Colonial Identity. *Romanticism*, 25(1), 81–89.

Sharpe, Jenny. (2002). *Ghosts of Slavery: A Literary Archeology of Black Women's Lives*. Minneapolis: University of Minnesota Press.

Shum, Matthew. (2009). The Prehistory of *The History of Mary Prince*: Thomas Pringle's "The Bechuana Boy." *Nineteenth-Century Literature*, 64(3), 291–322.

Siemerling, Winifred. (2015). *The Black Atlantic Reconsidered: Black Canadian Writing, Cultural History, and the Presence of the Past*. Montreal: McGill-Queen's University Press.

Simmons, Merinda K. (2009). Beyond "Authenticity": Migration and the Epistemology of "Voice" in Mary Prince's *History of Mary Prince* and Maryse Condé's *I, Tituba*. *College Literature*, 36(4), 75–99.

Stepto, Robert. (1991). *From Behind the Veil: A Study of Afro-American Narrative*. 2nd ed. Chicago: Chicago University Press.

Stoler, Ann Laura. (2001). Tense and Tender Ties: The Politics of Comparison in North American History and (Post) Colonial studies. *Journal of American History*, 88(3), 829–865.

Stouck, David. (1974). "Secrets of the Prison House": Mrs. Moodie and the Canadian Imagination. *Dalhousie Review*, 54, 463–472.

Sussman, Charlotte. (2000). *Consuming Anxieties: Consumer Protest, Gender, and British Slavery, 1713–1833*. Stanford: Stanford University Press.

Swan, Bradford F. (1970). *The Spread of Printing: The Caribbean Area*. London: Routledge.

Thomas, Christa Zeller. (2009). "I Had Never Such a Shed Called a House Before": The Discourse of Home in Susanna Moodie's *Roughing It in the Bush. Canadian Literature*, 203, 105–113.

Thomas, Helen. (2000). *Romanticism and Slave Narratives: Transatlantic Testimonies*. Cambridge: Cambridge University Press.

Thomas, Leah. (2019). Knowledge Networks: Contested Geographies in *The History of Mary Prince. Aphra Behn Online: Interactive Journal for Women and the Arts, 1640–1830*, 9(2), article 2. https://scholarcommons.usf.edu/abo/vol9/iss2/2/.

Thomas, Sue. (2005). *Pringle* v. *Cadell* and *Wood* v. *Pringle*: The Libel Cases over *The History of Mary Prince. Journal of Commonwealth Literature*, 40(1), 113–135.

Thurston, John. (1996). *The Work of Words: The Writing of Susanna Strickland Moodie*. Montreal: McGill-Queen's University Press.

Townsend, Mark. (2020). Home Office "Uses Racial Bias" When Detaining Immigrants. *The Guardian*. www.theguardian.com/politics/2020/jun/21/home-office-uses-racial-bias-when-detaining-immigrants?

Vigne, Randolph. (2011). *The South African Letters of Thomas Pringle*. Cape Town: Van Riebeck Society.

(2012). *Thomas Pringle: South African Pioneer, Poet and Abolitionist*. Woodbridge: Boydell & Brewer.

Warner, Ashton. (1831). *Negro Slavery Described by a Negro: Being the Narrative of A. W. With an Appendix Containing the Testimony of Four Christian Ministers. By S. Strickland*. London: Samuel Maunder.

Whitlock, Gillian. (2000). *The Intimate Empire: Reading Women's Autobiography*. London: Cassell.

Cambridge Elements $\equiv$

Eighteenth-Century Connections

Series Editors

Eve Tavor Bannet
University of Oklahoma

Eve Tavor Bannet is George Lynn Cross Professor Emeritus, University of Oklahoma and editor of *Studies in Eighteenth-Century Culture*. Her monographs include *Empire of Letters: Letter Manuals and Transatlantic Correspondence 1688–1820* (Cambridge, 2005), *Transatlantic Stories and the History of Reading, 1720–1820* (Cambridge, 2011) and *Eighteenth-Century Manners of Reading: Print Culture and Popular Instruction in the Anglophone Atlantic World* (Cambridge, 2017). She is editor of *British and American Letter Manuals 1680–1810* (Pickering & Chatto, 2008), *Emma Corbett* (Broadview, 2011) and, with Susan Manning, *Transatlantic Literary Studies* (Cambridge, 2012).

Rebecca Bullard
University of Reading

Rebecca Bullard is Associate Professor of English Literature at the University of Reading. She is the author of *The Politics of Disclosure: Secret History Narratives, 1674–1725* (Pickering & Chatto, 2009), co-editor of *The Plays and Poems of Nicholas Rowe, volume 1* (Routledge, 2017) and co-editor of *The Secret History in Literature, 1660–1820* (Cambridge, 2017).

Advisory Board

Linda Bree, Independent
Claire Connolly, University College Cork
Gillian Dow, University of Southampton
James Harris, University of St Andrews
Thomas Keymer, University of Toronto
Jon Mee, University of York
Carla Mulford, Penn State University
Nicola Parsons, University of Sydney
Manushag Powell, Purdue University
Robbie Richardson, University of Kent
Shef Rogers, University of Otago
Eleanor Shevlin, West Chester University
David Taylor, Oxford University
Chloe Wigston Smith, University of York
Roxann Wheeler, Ohio State University
Eugenia Zuroski, MacMaster University

About the Series

Exploring connections between verbal and visual texts and the people, networks, cultures and places that engendered and enjoyed them during the long Eighteenth Century, this innovative series also examines the period's uses of oral, written and visual media, and experiments with the digital platform to facilitate communication of original scholarship with both colleagues and students.

Cambridge Elements ≡

Eighteenth-Century Connections

Elements in the Series

Printed in the United States
by Baker & Taylor Publisher Services